SCOTLAND

A Concise History

B.C. to 1990

For Olive

SCOTLAND

A Concise History

B.C. to 1990

James Halliday

GORDON WRIGHT PUBLISHING
25 MAYFIELD ROAD, EDINBURGH EH9 2NQ
SCOTLAND

British Library Cataloguing in Publication Data
Halliday, James, *1927-*
    Scotland : a concise history.
    1. Scotland, history
    I. Title
    941.1

ISBN 0-903065-66-5

Cover Photograph of the Forth Bridges by Gordon Wright.

Typeset by Gordon Wright Publishing Ltd. Edinburgh.
Printed and Bound by Billing & Sons Ltd. Worcester.

Contents

Maps

Battle Plans

Family Lines

Foreword

Not so many years ago it was commonly argued that Scots could not really learn about their history because 'there are no books'. It was an absurdly untrue statement even then, and it is certainly untrue now. General histories, in single volumes or in multi-volume series, of scholarly quality, are now readily available and widely-studied. Studies of particular themes and topics, and edited collections of documents, are becoming available in such variety as to encourage the serious study of virtually all aspects of our history; and the Scottish universities have been fortunate in recent years to have the services of distinguished and influential historians working in the field of Scottish history, once the poor stepbairn of History departments.

These scholarly activities have stimulated many humbler works whose aim is to bring some knowledge of Scottish history to pupils and students at school or college, and to such members—and there are many—of the general public, who are awakening to an interest in Scotland's story.

Why then this book? It does not, and cannot, offer an exhaustive coverage of Scotland's history, nor would I have the impertinence to attempt such a task. I have tried to offer, to the general reader, not another narrative, but rather an explanation. I have concentrated upon what I believe to be the factors and the influences, the events and developments, the opinions and the decisions, which have caused Scots to undergo that set of experiences which we call our history.

James Halliday

The Author

James Halliday was born in Wemyss Bay in 1927. After attending the village school at Skelmorlie and Greenock High School, he graduated in history at Glasgow University, being awarded the Medley and Lanfine Prizes during his course.

He taught in Further Education at Ardeer and in High Schools in Coatbridge and Uddingston, before going to Dunfermline High School in 1958. There he was appointed Principal Teacher of History, leaving in 1967 to join the History Department of Dundee College of Education. In 1979 he became head of that department until retiring in 1988.

He was awarded the M. Litt. degree from Glasgow University in 1963 for his study of the issues and personalities of the Revolution in Scotland during the years 1688-90. He has served at various times on the council of the Scottish History Society, the Scottish Records Association and the Scottish Association of Teachers of History, and has written extensively on history and the teaching of the subject.

7

The Wallace Statue, Aberdeen. *(Photo: Valentines)*

The Land and the People

The land of Scotland has dictated what sort of history its people would have. The Scots have mountains and marshes; long, narrow, steep-sided glens, all too often open to north-west winds; acid soil and a climate which sees the seasons overlapping, the only certainty being that the growing season will be short. Here the Scots have had to do the best they could with what they had, and all through their history, with hard work and much ingenuity, they have managed to make the land serve its people better than might have been expected.

As well as the land there is the sea. No one in Scotland is very far from the sea, and even if the actual oceans are at some distance, there are long sea-lochs, their waters probing into the heart of the country, and there are rivers widening out into firths.

The sea and the lochs and the firths have often served as a defence—moats, as it were, behind which the Scots might shelter. But, important for strategy and defence as they were, these waters were also routes for trade and international contacts. The waters which were so often a barricade, could easily become roads, along which traders and administrators travelled to carry out their tasks. Until as recently as, say, 1960, the traditional and most convenient method of entry to towns and villages all along the shores of the west coast of the country and the western shores of the Firth of Clyde was by sea.

So, the nature of the land had largely determined how, and how successfully, the Scots would make their living and organise their activities. But in yet another respect their experiences were dictated by the residence which fate had given them. All through historic times the Scottish people have had to share an island with another people, far stronger than they in all respects—more numerous, more wealthy and usually more advanced technologically, especially in methods of warfare. Consciously and instinctively the Scots have always had to live with this fact, and their first and constant political problem has been how they might best co-exist with the English. Different solutions to this problem have been adopted at different times, or have been urged by competing Scottish factions at the same time. In either case the Scots have had to make up their minds whether their interests are best served by collaboration with English objectives and English power, and an acceptance of the fact of English dominance in Britain, or whether they should resist absorption, and make the preservation of their national identity a priority. It is the supporters of this latter policy who find grimly humorous accuracy in the remark of a Scottish writer in modern times that the Scots needed the Alps, but God had given them the Cheviots.

And what of the people of this land? Who are the Scots? Like any other people in modern times they are the descendants of every settler who ever lived here. They are a nation of immigrants, even though their immigrant ancestors came many centuries ago, some beyond recorded time. Humans came to Scotland, following the retreating ice some 8000 years ago. The earliest pioneering visitors were probably exactly that—visitors, from the European mainland, driven by hope and curiosity, by ambition and chance, to gather plants and hunt living things for food. In due course, no doubt, some of these visitors were content with what they had found, and saw the prospect of a satisfactory future in this newly found land. So they settled, not at first in any recognisable permanent communities, but living rather a nomadic life passing the days and years and generations in fishing and hunting along the shores, and sometimes entering, greatly daring, the forests of the interior. By 6000 years ago there were certainly permanent inhabitants who are the first ancestors of the Scots.

As time passed, later waves of visitors and settlers arrived, bringing with them new genes, new skills and new customs; adding to the ability of the natives to use implements of bone, wood and stone, the knowledge of metal-working in bronze and iron; offering as a means of livelihood not just hunting, gathering and herding, but crop growing—agriculture in the proper sense. Once the skills of seed-time and harvest were acquired; settlement in the real sense of permanent residence in selected sites was possible.

Our knowledge of how and when this sequence of events took place can never be wholly satisfactory, because all this happened before written records, and even before oral tradition can be used to fill the gap which the absence of written evidence leaves. Our one source of information is the science of archaeology. Archaeologists have done—and continue to do— wonders in providing the rest of us with our awareness of the remote past, but there are, inevitably, limits to what this can tell us. The identification of a site of historic interest is largely a matter of luck, however informed and perceptive the searcher may be; and the excavation of such a site is costly in time and money. We have to accept the evidence of the archaeologist in much the same way as one accepts the evidence of modern political scientists using samples to point to probabilities.

The sites discovered and excavated are the archaeologist's samples. From the shells and fish bones in the middens buried under the sands of Tentsmuir in Fife, we learn of the presence and survival methods of our earliest natives. From the discovery of a hollowed-out log or dugout canoe in the bed of the River Tay we deduce that men were able, using such vessels, to make sea-borne journeys. At the wonderful site of Skara Brae in Orkney we can see preserved the stone skeleton of a village, 4000 years old, buried under the sand by one gale, and laid bare by chance, after almost 4000 years, by another. From such sites we can learn what these ancestors of ours ate and wore; from the articles and ornaments found we can make deductions about their society; and when we find the graves where they buried their dead or their cremated ashes, we can even have a modest awareness of their beliefs.

We can use this kind of evidence to identify the variety of peoples, arriving at different times, because their goods are new and different and

The Ring of Brodgar, Stenness, Orkney. *(Photo: Gordon Wright)*

because their dead are buried in different fashion in tombs of different structure and dimensions. Even the poor exposed skeletons tell the story of a variety of peoples with differing physical characteristics, all of whom came to live here. We can begin to see, in the mind's eye, a kind of parade of the earliest, primitive hunters, the more skilled agriculturalists, and the metal-working Beaker folk, who buried their dead in individual tombs, leaving with each the vessels and implements which might be found useful in the after life which they obviously expected.

That there was a spiritual side to the life of all these people, the barrows and cists testify; as also, most of all, do the great stone circles like those at Brodgar in Orkney or Callanish in Lewis. These sites are signs of a conscious and deliberate decision, by people of whom we know so little, to raise symbols of honour and respect. As time passed these symbols came to bear carvings, proving that an artistic instinct had developed and was here revealed.

These then were our ancestors. They were not unique. Those who came here had come from somewhere else, and there they had left behind their kindred. The distinctiveness of the Scots is not therefore to be found in any one genetic origin, but rather in the blending of all these components which occurred here and, in these proportions, here alone.

We are inclined to form wrong impressions of what would happen as successive waves of invaders descended upon the people already in possession of the land. It is easy to assume that invaders would go in for

11

Pictish stone, Aberlemno, near Brechin. *(Photo: James Halliday)*

massacre and extermination, but a little commonsense should lead us to calmer and more accurate judgement.

For one thing, while some victims of the attack will die in heroic resistance, and others, more lucky, will run away, the vast majority simply stay where they are and make the best of a bad job. The conquerors, for their part, don't want corpses, they want workers, servants, perhaps slaves, but at least useful, living subordinates.

Also when conquest and occupation by intruders first happens, the intruders are almost by definition, warrior bands and thus male. As well as land and property, victorious men will seize upon women by right of conquest, and will claim them as their mates. After the initial attacks had occurred and a new dominant group had established itself, the future lay with people whose parentage was part native and part conqueror.

The conquerors, to be sure, would impose their kind of society, their customs, and, especially, their language; but they could not and did not eradicate the people they had conquered. They dominated and ruled, but that is not the same as destroying those now at their mercy.

We can see this pattern unfolding when we turn to consider the group of invaders who next came to Britain, because we are in a position to know much more about them than we can possibly know of the earliest peoples.

For knowledge of these earliest inhabitants we have to rely upon archaeology and scientific deductions, but the new invaders have left an oral and, eventually, a written record from which we can draw understanding.

These new invaders, arriving some 2500 years ago, were members of the Celtic racial group, coming from the north-western parts of Europe, and at least kindred of, if not wholly identical to, the Gauls who then held those lands. They were of the Brythonic branch of the Celtic peoples, or 'P' Celts, so called because their language commonly employed labial consonants, p, b, v and so on, in words like 'pen' = 'head' and 'ap' = 'son of'. They established their supremacy over the land and its existing inhabitants, becoming a kind of aristocracy and imposing their ways and their languages. The now subordinate natives, most of them, lived on, but their language did not. Only fragments of any pre-Celtic speech remain, particularly in place-names. (After all the oldest named things in the world are the mountains and rivers and other natural features upon which humans have looked since mankind's earliest days).

Of the people themselves we lose track, meeting them probably in the stories and legends of their Celtic conquerors. Celtic folk-lore is rich in stories of strange secret people, dwelling in remote parts of the country; secretive, furtive, shunning the daylight. These small, dark folk, brownies, elves, fairy folk, are probably the unassimilated survivors of the pre-Celtic peoples.

As for the Celts, they applied to themselves the name 'Pretani'. And when the next invaders arrived they seem to have heard the name and adopted it, with only a slight error in pronunciation, and called the people they found, 'Britoni'.

The new invaders, the Romans, were of course very different from previous settlers. In the first place they weren't really settlers at all, and had not been prompted to come to Britain by land hunger, ambition or flight from even more ferocious intruders into their own homelands. They were the masters of the European and Mediterranean world, and they came as masters to extend their power and assert their authority over one of the few parts of the world which they did not yet own. Their role was like that of governors and administrators, and commercial entrepreneurs; they had not come to farm or to work, merely to rule those who did.

They conquered and subdued the Celtic-ruled tribes, beginning in the south of the island and moving gradually north. By around 80 A.D. they were active as far north as the Solway and Tweed, and on the passes over the Cheviots. But the further north they went the more difficult it was to keep their legions supplied and controlled from their great depots and garrison centres at York and Chester.

In the year 80 A.D., the Roman governor, Julius Agricola, struck northwards from the Solway/Tyne line, and began a campaign intended no doubt to bring the northern tribes into the same degree of subjection as their kin in the south. Four main tribes stood in his path. In the east, between the Tweed and the Forth, were the Votadini, and their stronghold on Traprain Law. Westwards of there lay the territory of the Selgovae; and further west still, in the valley and estuary of the Clyde, were the Novantae and the Damnonii. Only the Selgovae appear to have sought seriously to obstruct Agricola's advance, and caused him to build what became a major fort, at Newstead—the Roman 'Trimontium', nestling as it did at the foot of the three peaks of the Eildon Hills.

The Eildon Hills from Scott's View. *(Photo: Gordon Wright)*

Traprain Law, East Lothian. *(Photo: Gordon Wright)*

With these tribes subdued, Agricola advanced further north, and controlled the Forth/Clyde isthmus with a line of forts. From this base in 84 A.D. he marched northwards, along the only route which geographical conditions then made feasible; across the Carron, then the Forth near the site of Stirling, in the territory of the Maeatae, and then to the Tay at its highest navigable point, present day Perth.

Beyond the Tay his legions moved northwards, his supply ships moving in parallel with his army, and making contact every so often to replenish supplies. Eventually his advance brought him to the spot, never yet acceptably indentified, called Mons Graupius. There the northern tribes, united it seems in resistance, stood at bay; and their leader Calgacus called on his men to resist to the last against the Romans and their plans which Calgacus saw would involve the ruin and destruction of their society. The Roman future he rejected, in the phrase which Tacitus has made famous, 'Where they make a desert, they call it "peace".

Agricola won the battle, but total conquest and occupation of the north proved beyond his capacity. The best he could do was to have small forts to keep watch at the north of the glens which gave access into and from the further mountain regions.

Before his term of duty ended he had constructed these outposts; the forts along the Forth and Clyde, and a network of forts and roads along which reinforcements and supplies could be brought as required. But the Roman presence in these parts was of short duration. The main Roman frontier from around 120 A.D. was defined by Hadrian's Wall, and north of that wall there was a very limited civilian presence. A final attempt was made by Lollius Urbicus, the Roman governor in 142-3 A.D., who tried to make a more substantial and permanent wall along the Forth/Clyde line, which was named the Antonine Wall in honour of the Roman emperor of the day. This wall was built of turf on a base of stone, and was some 14ft. wide. It had forts at roughly two-mile intervals along its length, and the most impressive signs of a settled Roman way of life are to be found at these strong points.

15

But the Romans did leave behind them, more important than roads and forts, baths and villas, the experience and the memory of Christianity. The earliest Christians in Britain were soldiers and their families, or officials serving the legions and their organisations in some capacity. There are Christian signs at several sites, dating from the earliest days of the Antonine Wall, and for over a century before Roman rule ended in Britain, the Empire had been officially Christian. For a few brief years in the mid-fourth century the area between the Walls was once more brought under Roman control, and during that period there was born, into a Christian society, the first known Christian evangelist in our history, St. Ninian.

Born in the Solway area, and educated, according to tradition, in Rome, the young Ninian spent time in the monastic community led by St. Martin near Tours. Returning home, some time before 400 A.D., he established his stone church 'Candida Casa' at Whithorn which served as a centre of missionary activity carried on by Ninian and his followers. So when we speak of Christianity being brought to Britain in the sixth century, by St. Columba or St. Augustine, we speak carelessly, and with thoughtless disregard for what was Rome's most profound legacy to our country.

There are limits, which should be obvious, to what walls can and cannot do. Separation over a period of generations can create differences in society, and even in speech, on either side of the wall which creates the separation. But in real essentials the people on either side remain as they were before the wall was built. If the wall is built through the lands of a single people, then biologically a single people they remain.

All people in Britain when the Romans arrived had a common ancestry, and retained it, regardless of any wall or action by the Romans. Sometimes the Latin writers mention, as a kind of alternative name for the Caledonians, 'the Picts', and much energy has been expended in seeking to answer the question 'Who were the Picts?'. The commonsense view has to be that the Picts were merely the Britons who had avoided incorporation into Rome's empire; and the Britons, throughout the island, were all the descendants of all who had gone before. Some differences there would be as a result of distances and isolation of one tribe from another; and very likely, pre-Celtic influences would survive more strongly in the part of the island than in another. Latin and English writers have led us into imagining some mysterious racial divisions where none really existed. The Wall separated people physically, when the sentries wished it to do so, but it could not undo the natural work of generations.

A useful corrective to these errors can be found in writing which is neither Latin nor English, but Welsh—the great epic *The Gododdin* which tells of the ride of the warriors of the Votadini—The Gododdin in other words—to the aid of their British kin at the great battle of Catraeth (Catterick). Kin all Britons still remained, and not the Antonine Wall, or even Hadrian's Wall, could alter that fact.

Not until post-Roman times did any new race intrude into the island, adding to the genetic pool of its people. In the latter years of the Roman occupation various raiders from overseas had carried out hit and run raids around the coasts. As Roman power declined the ability of its rulers to

16

provide for the defence of its remoter provinces lessened, until finally, after several forlorn attempts to avoid the decision, the legions were withdrawn from Britain altogether in 407 A.D..

The departure of the Romans meant that hit and run raiders might now find it possible—and tempting—to see themselves as settlers, and perhaps conquerors; and throughout the rest of the fifth century two such groups gradually established themselves in Britain.

From Scotia—the north eastern part of Hibernia (or Ireland)—came the Scots, a Celtic people like the Britons, but of a different branch of the family. They were Gaelic, not Brythonic, their speech categorised as 'Q'—Celt rather than 'P'—Celt, as they used guttural consonants—c, g—rather than the 'p' and 'b' of the earlier arrivals. Thus the Brythonic 'pen' is, in Gaelic, 'ceann', and 'ap' becomes 'mac'.

From Ireland access to the western coasts and islands of northern Britain was easy, and the journey no problem whatever to galley-borne fighting men. Scots over a period of time established settlements at various points throughout the inner Hebrides and around the sea lochs and firths; and by 500 they had arrived and concentrated in sufficient strength, to have created for themselves the Kingdom of Dalriada. This land had been until its seizure, the home of British/Pictish tribes, and was no doubt looked upon as national territory by the Pictish Kings. So, there would be anger and battles as the Scots sought to penetrate further inland, and the resentful Picts sought to keep them out. On the evidence of surviving place-names we can see a pattern to the eventual extent of the Scottish conquest. Obviously there was no clearly defined boundary, such as modern states would establish, but the Scottish advance can be seen to have halted along the high ground known anciently as 'Drumalban' where modern Argyle meets the shires of Inverness and Perth.

In the generations which followed, Scottish power and influence moved gradually east and north east, carried forward often no doubt, by war, but owing much to the work and influence of the first truly historical Scot, St. Columba.

Columba—Columcille in his own language—was a prince of the royal house in Irish Dalriada, who had to leave his home after a dispute over, so tradition tells us, the copying of a Christian psalter. The dispute had caused bloodshed, and blame seems to have been laid upon Columba who left Ireland for exile in Scottish Dalriada in 563. There, on the island of Iona, already a traditional place of Christian worship, he and his group of followers made their home and began the mission work which made the little island one of the most influential and loved centres of Christendom.

As well as being a Christian evangelist Columba was also a Scot, and, we may guess, a patriotic one. His fellow-Scots had only recently suffered a defeat in the long-running war with the Picts. Perhaps if the Pictish king could be won over to Christianity like the Scots, enmity between the two would diminish and harmony prevail. Possibly with this part-religious part-diplomatic purpose, Columba and a few colleagues (two of them themselves Picts) set off along the Great Glen to meet and negotiate with the Pictish King Brude at Inverness.

17

This mission was successful, and a shared Christian affiliation now promised better relations between Picts and Scots. For the rest of his life Columba, and the followers whom he taught and inspired, carried their mission and this Scottish influence into much of Pictland, including Orkney and the Western Isles. He also established friendly contacts with fellow-Christians in British territory south of the Clyde, inheritors of the tradition begun by St. Ninian, especially St. Mungo (or Kentigern) who, we are told, received Columba as a visitor in Glasgow in 584.

By the time of his death in 597 Columba had served his faith with great devotion and success, but he had also proved a wise counsellor to the Scottish Kings of Dalriada and his legacy to his fellow countrymen was political as well as religious.

Britons and Picts were more or less the same people by blood at least, with the latter perhaps retaining slightly more traces of their pre-Celtic ancestors. The Scots were more distantly related, but still related. But in the dying days of Roman Britain there appeared around the coasts yet another wave of invaders, with no ancestral or cultural ties to the Britons at all. These were the English—known variously as Angles, Saxons and Jutes—who first established themselves in the south and south-eastern coastal areas of Britain. Their settlements gradually extended along the east coast, as later fleets brought over more settlers from their German homelands; and by 597 there was an English stronghold north of Hadrian's Wall, at Bamborough.

As English power grew, and strongholds established links with one another, by around 590 they had cut a corridor right across the island from the North Sea to the Irish sea, separating the Britons of the north from their brothers in what became Wales. Their northern expansion brought them into war against an alliance of Britons and Scots; and the English victory at Degsastane (possibly near Jedburgh) in 603 gave them control of the eastern coast as far north as the Forth.

The eastern boundary was for the moment well-defined; but there was no necessity to imagine that the Forth must be the river along which Pict and Englishman would bristle at each other. The border might move south to the Tweed, or the Tyne or the Wear—perhaps even the Humber. On the other hand it might move north to the Tay or the Moray Firth.

On the west, the question was whether the Britons might succeed in re-uniting, or whether at least they might hold the whole area north of the line of the Ribble. The alternative was that the English might widen their corridor, and push the boundary to the Solway or even to the Clyde.

The crucial fact however was that the English had succeeded in cutting off the native-cum-Celtic peoples in the north of the island from their kindred in the west and south-west. As it turned out this division was never to be reversed. The future fate of the sundered sections was to be very different and the northern section was in due course to emerge as Scotland.

Early Kings of Alba

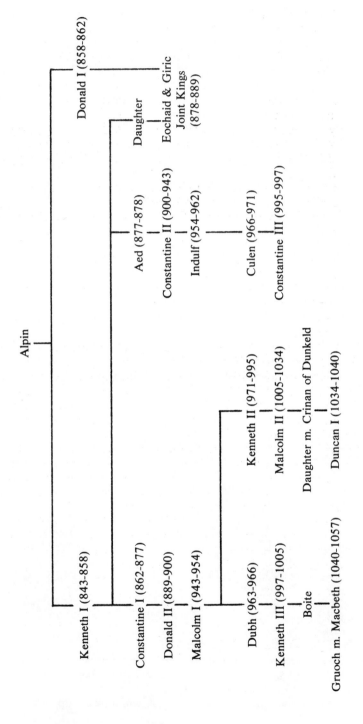

Alpin

Kenneth I (843-858)

Donald I (858-862)

Daughter

Eochaid & Giric
Joint Kings
(878-889)

Aed (877-878)

Constantine II (900-943)

Indulf (954-962)

Culen (966-971)

Constantine III (995-997)

Constantine I (862-877)

Donald II (889-900)

Malcolm I (943-954)

Dubh (963-966)

Kenneth II (971-995)

Malcolm II (1005-1034)

Daughter m. Crinan of Dunkeld

Duncan I (1034-1040)

Kenneth III (997-1005)

Boite

Gruoch m. Macbeth (1040-1057)

Making a Kingdom

The raw materials from which Scotland was constructed were three Kingdoms—Pictland, Dalriada and 'Strathclyde' (as the northern lands of the Britons came to be known), with the addition of outlying parts of two larger kingdoms—Lothian (the part of English Northumbria which lay between Tweed and Forth); and the Hebrides, the Western Isles, which were part of the great sea borne empire of the Norwegians.

Pictland was the largest of the Kingdoms and, one would have thought, the most populous and powerful. But the Picts had had the ill-fortune to be victims of attacks by all their neighbours at one time or another.

Their resistance to the encroaching Scots, and the defeat which the growth of Dalriada implied, must have contributed to the weakening of Pictish power. As if the Scots were not problem enough, the Picts were later the target for English incursions. They proved strong and resolute enough to destroy the English threat for many years to come by winning, in 689, the great battle of Nechtansmere at Dunnichen near Forfar. The most deadly blows to the Picts however, came from the greatest fighting force in Northern Europe—the Norsemen or the 'Vikings'.

Sometimes the Vikings came as raiders, sometimes as settlers; and the grip which they established around the northern extremities of Britain and its adjacent islands was so strong and enduring that in place names and surnames the memory survives to this day. The towns and villages of Caithness—Scrabster, Lybster, Ulbster—bear names which testify to their Norse antecedents. Sutherland was 'Southern land' to the men from the North; and throughout the Hébrides place names ending in '-bost' or '-nish' or '-val' tell us that the Vikings lingered here. Among the people of the Western Isles to this day, Norse surnames ending in '-son' are fully as common as Gaelic 'macs'.

All through these northern and western seas, firths and lochs prowled the Norse galleys, bringing at one time civil and good-humoured trade, at another permanent settlement and frequently destruction and slaughter. 'From the fury of the Northmen O dear Lord deliver us' was one prayer long-used along the western shores. The Norse were pagan during the early years of their marauding, and churches and churchmen suffered cruelly at their hands—or at least feared they might. This fear undoubtedly prompted the departure from Iona of many of its people and the transfer of relics, treasures and religious focus from Iona to, especially, Dunkeld, in Perthshire and even to Kells in Ireland.

The Britons of Strathclyde and the Scots alike had learned to flee from the raven banners, but the brunt of these attacks was borne by the Picts. In 839 they suffered a particularly disastrous defeat at the hands of the Norsemen, and the King of Scots, Kenneth MacAlpin, took the opportunity to attack the afflicted Picts and, by 843, make himself their King. It is possible—even probable—that Kenneth was in the line of descent from Pictish kings, as inter-marriage linking the two royal lines appears to have happened on numerous occasions over the generations. It is probable that the role of Kenneth has been emphasised rather more than it should, but the tradition which has come down through centuries, that he was the first king of a united Pictland and Dalriada is unlikely ever to be entirely rejected.

Another tradition, perhaps ill-founded but none the less interesting, tells us that kingship among the Picts did not pass from father to son, but from a deceased king to the son of a sister—his nephew, or to the son of his mother—his brother. In other words, though men ruled in Pictland, their eligibility to rule depended upon their female parentage. Such a custom, though exceedingly uncommon, was not unknown elsewhere; and it is not to be dismissed as absurd. On the contrary, only by some such procedure could kingship be kept, beyond any shadow of doubt, in a royal line. There is, after all, never any possible doubt (other than in the event of deliberate deception) as to the identity of a child's mother, whereas the identity of the other parent has to be taken on trust.

Certainly the passing of the crown back and forth seems more regular than would justify the alternative explanation of feud and murder.

At all events, in 843 Kenneth emerges as first beyond-doubt king of a united Scottish/Pictish kingdom, Alba, which has been described as 'the only kingdom of significance in the otherwise fragmented Celtic world'.

Just as we must doubt that the union of Picts and Scots was effected in such a tidy, swift fashion, so also the traditional explanation as to how this new kingdom came to absorb lands to the south, as far as the present Scottish border, is not quite the whole story.

In the east, south of the Forth, lay territory under the control in theory of the English Kings of Bernicia, later part of the powerful kingdom of Northumbria. But these lands between Tweed and Forth, were at the outer limits of Northumbrian power. That power was in any case weakened from time to time by wars and divisions among the English kingdoms and principalities. (Centuries later the Scots amused themselves by jeering at the English on the grounds that Scotland had been a united country at a time when England was divided among seven kings). As a result kings of Scots, from time to time, were able to exercise power and authority in the area which was beginning to be known by its own particular name—Lothian.

In 1018 England, which had achieved a degree of internal unity but had then suffered the conquest of its northern half by the Danes, found itself at a disadvantage when the Scottish king, Malcolm II, took his army across the Tweed and defeated the army which the English from the Tyne and Tees valleys mustered against him. This Battle of Carham proved more final than might have been expected, and the eastern border between England and its northern neighbour, remains today, along the River Tweed.

In the west, the kings of Alba came to exercise increasing domination over the British kingdom of Strathclyde or Cumbria. It seems to have been the custom for the kings of Alba to appoint their chosen successors to be, in

The Tweed Bridge at Coldstream links Scotland and England. *(Photo: Gordon Wright)*

title, kings of Strathclyde, but in a position of dependence upon the larger kingdom. Malcolm II appointed his grandson, Duncan, King of Strathclyde, but Duncan, largely by chance, was also the sole real contender for the crown of his grandfather. So, in 1034, Duncan, King of Strathclyde, inherited the throne of the larger kingdom also, and the ancient British kingdom was incorporated into a new united monarchy with its border placed at least as far south as the Solway.

Thus by 1034 we can begin to speak of the kingdom of Scotland, and picture it as having virtually the border which exists today. The only lands which remained to be brought under the Scottish crown were the islands and parts of the Scottish mainland where the Norse still ruled.

A united country, such as might be expected in modern times, was hardly to be looked for in the eleventh century. Unity shows itself in easy and competent administration by rulers whose orders are obeyed, and whose plans are implemented. But administration could not be easy when instructions had to be carried by individuals from one point to another; when the swiftest means of transport available was a horse; when there was nothing equivalent to a police force making travel reasonably safe, and when the ultimate power—armed force—was available not just to the king, but to many of his subordinates as well. Also, it was not so easy for the Scottish kings to establish and assert their superiority over all others in the realm as it was, for instance, for the kings of England after 1066. In that year, by right of conquest William I was able to claim possession of the totality of English land, which he could then re-allocate in return for service and good behaviour. The Scottish kings never enjoyed this clean slate experience, but had, from the earliest days, to maintain authority by their own abilities.

Then, in addition to these technical obstacles to smooth government, there were recurring factional disputes. From the earliest days of full Scottish unity—the beginning of Duncan's reign in 1034—this basic disunity was revealed, with the challenge to Duncan's title and his defeat and death at the hands of Macbeth. It is now widely understood that Macbeth acted not as some sort of bandit chief, but as the representative of one long enduring faction among the various branches of the Royal family.

Two such branches had been excluded from hopes of royal office through the various brutalities of Kenneth II and his son Malcolm II, who made it their business to remove any rivals from their path. Macbeth may have taken it upon himself to act as champion of one of those excluded lines; and his strength was based on the lands of that particular family in Moray and the north-east generally. This fact suggests that the feud went far back even into the days of Dalriada, when one family or tribe of Scots was long in competition with another. Whatever the origins of conflict were, Macbeth did oust Duncan, and reigned for seventeen not unsuccessful years, before his own defeat and death at the hands of Duncan's son, Malcolm III.

Yet, the essential idea of unity remained, and no claimant or rebel was bent upon dismantling the Scottish kingdom as it had come to exist. Scottish unity was, by modern standards, no doubt less than perfect, but it was as genuine and as effective as the unity of any other kingdom at the time, where administrative problems were no less difficult and the emergence of claimants to the throne no less frequent.

Malcolm III is most commonly known not by his numeral but by a nickname 'Canmore'. This name, from the Gaelic *Ceann mor,* is literally translated as 'big-head'. The term may have been used because of his physical appearance, but it has sometimes been suggested that the term may have been used in a symbolic sense, and really means 'great chief', or implies 'great wisdom'.

Certainly Malcolm is usually thought of as one of Scotland's great monarchs, though, when we examine the actual events of his reign, we must wonder why. Perhaps his reputation stands high simply because he was the first king to rule a united Scotland with limits more or less those of today. Perhaps it stems from the fact that his reign was long (1057-1093); but perhaps his reputation has gained from the fact that he was on the throne when events and changes of great importance occurred.

In terms of actual achievement there is really little to enthuse over. With his two powerful neighbours—Norway and England—he began on good terms. He owed his victory in Scotland to Earl Siward's English army, after all, and gratitude towards England might have been expected. His ties with Norway, or, at least, the Norse warrior leaders with power in and near Scotland, were established by his marriage with Ingibiorg, the widow of the great Earl Thorfinn of Orkney. But, if Malcolm's plans were of peace and co-operation, they very soon began to go wrong.

The throne of England passed from the ancient royal house of Wessex, on the death of Edward the Confessor, firstly to a king by appointment rather than by descent, Earl Harold of Wessex; and shortly thereafter to the conquering Duke William of Normandy. This conquest sent rightful

The Four Kingdoms

NORSE

PICTLAND

DALRIADA

Moray Firth

Firth of Lorne

Firth of Tay

Firth of Forth

Antonine Wall

LOTHIAN

STRATHCLYDE

Firth of Clyde

Hadrian's Wall

Solway Firth

claimants to the English throne into exile—an experience with which some of them had been already familiar when Danish kings ruled early in the eleventh century. The main claimant was Edgar, who sought refuge with his two sisters, Margaret and Christina, at King Malcolm's court. Malcolm must have been by this time (1068) a widower, and promptly determined that Margaret should now be his wife. The English refugees were in no position to refuse, and the marriage was duly celebrated, probably in Dunfermline, which Malcolm had made one of his most frequently used residences.

All sorts of consequences followed from the marriage. It obviously placed Malcolm among the enemies of the new king and regime in England, with, finally, disastrous consequences. In the meantime, and for the rest of his reign, the influence wielded by Queen Margaret and her following was profound. And, even after Malcolm's death, Margaret's influence endured, as one after another, three of her sons followed Malcolm, their father, as kings of Scotland.

Malcolm was killed, together with his eldest son, in 1093 by an English ambush as he was returning from a military raid into England, and Margaret died within days of hearing the news. In Scotland the throne was taken by Malcolm's brother Donald, whose power was then challenged by Duncan, son of Malcolm by his first marriage, who had been at the English court as a hostage for several years, but who was now employed by King William II of England as a potential puppet king. Duncan's power in Scotland was brief. He was acknowledged as King Duncan II in May 1094, but was murdered in November of the same year, enabling power to pass to his uncle, Donald III, who enjoyed the support of the eldest surviving son of Malcolm and Margaret, Edward. The younger children of Margaret once more sought refuge in England, and it was the turn of the eldest of those refugees, Edgar, to be the new client of the English king. In 1097 an English army defeated Donald and Edward and placed Edgar on the Scottish throne. Donald was blinded and imprisoned for life, while Edward, perhaps as a virtual prisoner, ended his days as a monk far in the south of England.

So Margaret's son Edgar reigned; and after him his younger brother Alexander, and, after Alexander, the youngest brother David. All three—especially perhaps, David—were very much their mother's sons, and Queen Margaret's influence, through them, left permanent marks upon Scotland.

Margaret is remembered particularly for her concern for religion and the church. Twice, at least, events in Europe had created a breach between the continent and the outlying islands of Britain and Ireland. The English, on their first coming, were pagan, and the Christian leaders in Ireland and in the various kingdoms of Scotland, were cut off from direct access to Rome and the papacy.

Later, unbroken Roman supervision of the church from central Europe to Ireland, was shattered once more by the success of the pagan Danes who by the ninth century had conquered the north and midlands of England. So, once more Ireland and Scotland had been left to some extent to develop away from close and regular contact with the controlling centres of the

Stained glass window, St. Margaret's Chapel, Edinburgh Castle. *(Photo: Gordon Wright)*

church in Europe. Naturally over the years, little local peculiarities crept in, and ideas and practices unknown to Rome evolved in Scotland.

Margaret was a cosmopolitan. By blood a daughter of the English royal house, she was born while her parents were in flight from the Danish kings (who once more, briefly, controlled England in the early eleventh century) and had found refuge in Hungary, recently Christianised by St. Stephen.

In the atmosphere of enthusiastic piety inevitably following this experience, Margaret grew up; and her adult life was dominated by her preoccupation with Christian work and order.

To her, the various differences which she found among the clergy in Scotland were unacceptable, and she made it her business to restore the church in Scotland to the full observance of Roman authority. Her models and guides were men of austerity and discipline. The monks who were summoned to establish a monastery at Dunfermline, were Benedictines; and gradually she and the churchmen who enjoyed her support, cleansed the Mass of various intrusions which had crept in; revived observance in proper form of Church festivals, and restored the pattern of organisation in dioceses, which had been apparently modified by monastic-style activity during the years of comparative isolation.

In practical ways, as well as in matters of doctrine and conduct, she assisted the church in its work. A chapel was built on the castle rock in Edinburgh; a 'Queen's ferry' was provided across the River Forth, to encourage the journey of pilgrims from south and west to St. Andrews, and, giving honour where it was due, she secured the restoration and revival of the sacred site of Iona.

She was, however, far from being unworldly. She had a highly developed idea of royal dignity— 'queenly as well as saintly' one writer has called her—and the court of King Malcolm was more cultured, more luxurious and more formal than it had previously been. A higher standard of living at court, and a closer association with the continental forms of religion both tended to encourage commercial contacts, and from the activities of merchants new standards of elegance and culture were derived.

One aspect of these wider contacts, however, had great significance. For whatever reason—family memories, ease of access, personal acquaintance, all no doubt contribute—Margaret tended to find her consultants in, or by way of, England. She was not the first, nor by any means the only, Scottish public figure who acted on the assumption that any influences reaching Scotland from the outside world would normally and properly pass through England first.

But of course England now was not English politically any more. Power and social influence were Norman, even though the mass of the people remained English or, in the north, half-Danish. So, when Margaret, her husband and her sons, entered into any sort of co-operation with the court at Westminster they were dealing with Norman kings, Norman officials, Norman courtiers and Norman churchmen.

There was so much to admire in the Normans. They had won England thanks to superior military techniques. They had brought to the country an efficiency of administration, and a competence in organisation, which was new and admirable. With the power which military victory gave them, they had imposed a pattern upon society which, if not previously unknown, had not been fully accepted until the post-conquest years.

This pattern, known to all later generations as the feudal system, was based upon tenure and use of land exercised by permission of the King. Society was contractual. Acceptance of royal authority was rewarded by the grant of land, which was then held as long as obedience was given in return.

There was nothing particularly intellectual in Duke William's use of this method of binding his subjects to him. All who had shared in the adventure of the Conquest expected to find themselves rewarded by generous grants of property. Indeed in few cases was there any other motive for their arrival in England at all. William had to reward his followers, but in doing so he made them his agents, his garrison as it were, policing the country through them and the military strongholds which they made of their dwellings. The Normans had come to rule and enjoy the fruits of power. The conquered would hew the wood and draw the water.

A Scottish king too had already shown that he appreciated what Normans had to offer a leader who could promise them rewards. The first Norman knights to come to Scotland came at the invitation of Macbeth. As it turned out they had backed the losing side on that occasion, but the idea was not forgotten.

Building a State

A good case could be made for regarding David I as the most significant and greatest king ever to rule in Scotland. His long reign 1124-53 saw the country undergo what one historian has called 'an explosion of new ideas, policies and practices'.

He is traditionally most famous on two counts; firstly that he brought into Scotland numerous Norman knights to whom he gave generous land grants, creating virtually a new aristocracy; and secondly, that he presided over the spectacular growth in the wealth, property and influence of the church.

He obviously saw in the Normans qualities from which government and society might have been expected to benefit. The oldest surviving charter of his reign is that which grants the lands of Annandale to Robert de Brus, whose family origins were in the Cotentin area of Normandy. Similar land grants were made to families like the Comyns, the Balliols, Lindsays and Grahams—all of them providing personalities of significance in later years. In his court and councils, these new men were prominent. Walter Fitzalan, son of a Breton family, became Steward, with extensive lands in Renfrewshire and central Ayrshire; and his descendants, taking his official position as a family name, became the Stewarts who were to rule Scotland, and England too, in due course.

Other important and enriching foreign influences were introduced by the religious orders which also gained from David's generosity.

Before he became king, David had invited a group of Augustinian canons to establish themselves as a community in Selkirk. Their venture was successful, and they moved to new quarters in Jedburgh in 1118. They were the trailblazers. In 1128 Tironensians came to Kelso, and another Augustinian house was established near Edinburgh Castle. These canons were particularly devoted to the veneration of the relics of the true cross, and their new headquarters, dedicated accordingly, was named Holyrood. In 1136 members of the great Cistercian Order were invited to come from Rievaulx in Yorkshire to take possession of new lands centring on Melrose; while in 1150 the latest and, in the eyes of many, the most beautiful of the abbeys of the east Borders, was founded at Dryburgh as a home for Premonstratensian monks.

Where the king led, subjects followed, and landowners endowed religious houses like Dundrennan and Sweetheart Abbeys in the west Borders.

These monasteries and abbeys grew and prospered, as did the communities around them—the Cistercians were always famed for their skill in estate and land management—and they were able in turn to establish branches, as it were, often far from their original base. Thus Melrose had colonies at Newbattle and Coupar Angus, while Kelso was mother house to later houses at Kilwinning, Arbroath and Lindores.

Dryburgh Abbey. *(Photo: Gordon Wright)*

The economic and cultural influence of these developments was immense and gave to Scotland new international contacts as the influx of Norman landowners had done. There was, of course, one snag. The lands given by David to Norman knights and the religious orders, had come, in most cases, from land previously in the possession of the crown. The time was to come when the wealth and property of the Church exceeded that of the monarchs, one of whom remarked bitterly that though King David was doubtless a saint, he was 'a sair saint to the crown'.

The new landowners and the new church foundations might fairly be seen as tending to internationalise and modernise the country. This claim can certainly be made for another of David's devices—the burghs.

Villages and towns, if they grow and develop naturally, do so for a variety of reasons. In each of the royal estates there was always some point at which the king might reside from time to time, and to that point were brought the supplies which all the local tenants were obliged to provide as their rent. Often the king was not even in residence; or at times there would be more produce than he and his court required, and the surplus would be disposed of, offered for sale or exchange in a kind of market.

The advantages of a market are always quickly obvious to any community. Trading—buying and selling—is the basis of any kind of economy which rises above mere self-sufficiency. Markets attracted customers, and customers were quickly seen as being ready to pay for the privilege of setting up their stalls, and the king was able to ask that a kind of toll or rental should be paid to him by each trader. Later, the king could adjust matters slightly by giving to the citizens of these market towns the right to charge these tolls for themselves, paying the crown an annual or regular fee for this privilege.

Similar developments occurred in villages near to a castle, or an abbey, or a monastery and were especially to be expected around a harbour, or at a point on a river which could be reached by sea-borne trading vessels, or a point at which the river could be crossed by ford or bridge. Important Scottish towns have their origins in these developments, Perth and Stirling for instance, on Tay and Forth; or Aberdeen, Dundee and Berwick on the coast.

Over all this activity David presided, governing with efficiency, using methods which he had learned from the Normans. The country was, for the most part, divided anew into units called counties, which a royal official, the Sheriff, would supervise. The Sheriffs and their counties came under the further supervision of the king's Justiciar; and royal castles were built at key points, where they did not already exist, to provide the administrative and military centres from which the Sheriffs and the Justiciar could work.

Scotland under King David was powerful, even in relation to Norman England; and for most of David's reign Scotland's border with England lay further south than before or since, along the Tees in the East and incorporating the ancestral lands of Cumbria. In addition David had gained, by his marriage to the daughter of a former English Earl of Northumbria, extensive lands in the east midlands of England—Huntingdon, Bedford and Northampton. These lands were obviously valuable to the king, but his possession of them set on foot a series of events which in the long run brought disaster upon his people.

Like anyone else holding lands in England, David did so as a subordinate or vassal to a superior—the King of England. Feudal land-holding involved a degree of ceremonial; and regularly, nobles and knights had to present themselves before their king to swear loyalty—fealty—and do homage. The ceremony involving kneeling in a defenceless and submissive pose, intended to show the inferiority of the person performing the ritual. David knelt, at one time or another, before Henry I and Stephen, and his successors in their turn did homage for the family lands in England. *They* all knew, of course, that the person kneeling there was the Earl of Huntingdon. To the eyes of the English kings and courtiers, the various Earls of Huntingdon looked remarkably like the Kings of Scots. Kings of England had cherished the notion that they were somehow superior to the Scottish kings, and had some title to their obedience. Malcolm III for instance, had submitted to William I at Abernethy in 1072 and to William II in 1091. These submissions, however, were in reality admissions of temporary military defeat, and the Scots kings had not yielded to the English notion that Britain held one real king—the King of England—and a variety of lesser, so-called kings including the King of Scots. But whether the King of Scots took it seriously or not, the repeated acts of homage, performed over a long period of time gave to the English kings an assurance of their right to control not just Huntingdon but Scotland as well.

One historian has written of King David, 'He had found Scotland an isolated cluster of small half-united states, barely emergent from the Dark Ages; he left her a kingdom, prosperous, organised, in the full tide of medieval life, and fully part of Europe, as she remained through the rest of the middle ages and some time after'. To write this is perhaps rather to under-estimate the preparatory work begun by David's parents and brothers, but it is certainly true that he had raised Scottish importance to a new and much higher level than before.

Not only did Scotland now exist as a very respectable little kingdom in the eyes of the outside world, but at home too David had created a new unity. This was displayed when his son, Henry, died in 1152, leaving three boys who were now David's heirs. David acted quickly, having the eldest of his three grandsons, Malcolm, taken on a royal tour around the kingdom, where he was everywhere presented and acknowledged as David's successor. Within the year David was dead, but he had done his work well, and his grandson came to rule as Malcolm IV with no serious challenge.

The reigns of David's two grandsons, Malcolm IV and William, contrasted in some respects very greatly. Malcolm reigned for only twelve years, dying young, unmarried and childless. William enjoyed the longest reign of any Scottish king—forty-nine years—and left four legitimate children to provide for the succession.

William'the Lion', a man of action rather than subtlety, unwisely drifted into war with Henry II of England. In the confused pattern of marches and skirmishes which followed, William was surprised and captured by an English force.

Having the King of Scots physically in his clutches, Henry was able to dictate terms. At Falaise, in Normandy, as a prisoner, William had to give his formal assent to the longstanding, but never admitted, claim of the English kings to be the feudal overlords of the Scottish monarchs. This treaty of 1174 was never to be forgotten by the English, and it coloured relations between the two countries for as long as Scotland survived.

So, in a sense, William's reign was disastrous for Scotland, opening the way to centuries of war and suffering. He bought back his status in 1189, paying Richard I the equivalent of a ransom in return for cancelling the Treaty of Falaise, but no matter that Richard made this bargain, later English kings when the chance arose, simply acted as though William's submission at Falaise stood for all time.

For the rest of his reign William governed Scotland with reasonable success; putting down a northern rising which had attracted Norwegian support, chartering more burghs—including Glasgow—and founding new religious houses, notably the abbey at Arbroath, where in 1214 King William was buried.

His son, Alexander II, found himself involved in the English baronial action against King John, which culminated in John's reluctant acceptance of Magna Carta in 1215; and the King of Scots was one of those whose grievances John promised to redress. At one point it even looked as though the rebel barons might choose Alexander as an alternative king to John, but their choice fell upon Louis of France instead, and Alexander's chance of spectacular professional advancement was gone. He had, in later years, a very up and down relationship with John's son Henry III, but his energies were mainly employed in dealing with domestic troubles.

Galloway and Moray, and their various local ruling families and factions,

Arbroath Abbey, burial place of William the Lion and site of the Declaration of Arbroath in 1320. *(Photo: Gordon Wright)*

were still capable of mischief. Alexander employed a tactic, which later kings were to use also; having found an apparently loyal supporter in these restless areas, he then gave that supporter responsibility for maintaining good order in the future. Thus in the north the Earl of Ross acted as the king's strong right arm and in Moray he fostered the power of the Comyn Earls of Buchan. Another branch of the Comyns played a similar role in Galloway, where they later became closely connected with another family whose influence was to grow in the area—the Balliols.

Also, Alexander had to meet unrest and violence along the western coast, where from time to time the kings of Norway, seeking to make more effective their control over the Hebrides, would incite, or at least take advantage of, local disturbances. To deal with such a threat, in 1249, Alexander led an expedition which succeeded in bringing Argyle under royal control; but, whatever plans Alexander may have had to extend his authority into the islands, he did not live to carry them out, dying on the Island of Kerrera, near Oban, with his work incomplete.

The accession to the throne of an eight-year-old boy, Alexander III, might at other times have been expected to mean disunity, intrigue and weakness in the governing of Scotland. But as it turned out, the unity and sense of common purpose developing from the days of David I, proved sufficiently strong for the child-king's status to be accepted without challenge and for the affairs of the kingdom to be conducted efficiently by committees of officials, nobles and churchmen until Alexander took effective personal control at the comparatively advanced age of twenty. Given the later reputation of Scottish nobles and courtiers for greed and treachery, their behaviour in the decade after 1249 is quite remarkable.

Such intrigue as did carry with it any threat of serious mischief came from King Henry III of England, whose shifty and conspiratorial nature prompted him to attempt to draw advantage from the presence of a child ruler in the neighbouring kingdom.

Henry had been in a position to influence the Scottish monarchy since Alexander II had married his sister; such marriages after all were intended precisely to create closer ties and interchange of influence between the families and realms of the two partners. However, the influence of Henry and English power upon Scotland had ended with the death of Queen Joan, and Alexander II's re-marriage to Marie de Coucy, mother of Alexander III. No doubt Henry now saw the possibility of re-asserting his powers in relation to Scotland, and thus swiftly arranged for the marriage of his daughter Margaret to the young Alexander.

So in December 1251 Alexander and his leading courtiers travelled to York, where on Christmas Day Alexander was knighted by the English king and on the following day was married to that king's daughter.

It would appear that Henry made an immediate attempt to benefit from the happy occasion, accepting Alexander's homage for his lands in England, and going on swiftly and smoothly, to invite the boy to do homage for his kingdom as well. It may be that Alexander was quick-witted and shrewd far beyond his years; it may be that his advisers had coached him well in what he might expect in York. In any case, astonishing though it may appear, the eleven-year-old Alexander responded that he had come to be married, not to deal with such serious matters of state policy, on which he could not speak without proper discussion with his Council.

Alexander and the kingdom had both been well-served during the years of his minority by the various men and groups who wielded power during those years. The whole period is distinguished by an unexpected political maturity. The Comyn and the Durward factions seemed able to live together and work together, sometimes in control, sometimes not, but neither group was treasonous in its purposes, and both, when in power, administered with whatever competence they could command. It seemed as though the work of Malcolm III and David I had at last been crowned with success, and that stability would be the kingdom's reward.

Alexander himself behaved with confidence and skill. He appointed to his Council the leaders of both major political groups, thus emphasising the fact of unity. The young king and his advisers presided over a period of economic advance, which they consciously encouraged. Burghs grew in importance and increasing trade brought growing prosperity. One Scottish burgh and port—Berwick—was handling trade worth 25 per cent of the total trade of England; on the land, arable acreage and production increased considerably, raising living standards of the people as a result; and trade and agriculture alike were encouraged and protected by the competence of Alexander's administration. Law and order—always necessary for economic confidence—were guaranteed by the work of Sheriffs in the various burghs and shires; of justiciars in larger areas, and by the king himself, who travelled regularly and extensively around the country.

The one external threat to security which Alexander II had not been able to remove before his death, was that posed by the remaining Norse presence in the Western Isles and the constant possibility that a vigorous Norwegian monarch might choose to breathe new life into Norse ambitions. Just such a crisis developed as Alexander took personal charge of his kingdom. He began by offering to buy the Norse-held islands from the Norwegian crown, and when his offer met with no favour, he allowed attacks by local Scots leaders to be made against the more accessible parts of the Norse territory. The Norwegian king Haakon, a man of immense character and prestige, was not likely to allow such challenges to go unpunished, and in 1263 he led a great fleet and army to restore the diminished power of Norway in the Scottish outposts of its empire, and to compel more submissive behaviour from Alexander.

Haakon's fleet sailed, reaching Lerwick in the Shetland Isles by the middle of July. By August he was gathering with his subordinates and supporters at Skye and in the Firth of Lorne. The reinforced—but delayed—Haakon sailed for Kintyre and into the Firth of Clyde. The Island of Arran was occupied and Bute overrun, while Scots and Norwegians talked terms of peace at Ayr. As the talks went on, the year advanced and the weather became more unsuitable for seaborne armies.

On 30 September westerly gales began to cause damage to Haakon's fleet, anchored between the Island of Cumbrae and the Ayrshire coast. The crews and warriors, on galleys driven ashore, were attacked by the Scottish local forces under Alexander the Steward; and throughout 1 and 2 October, skirmishes took place along the shore at Largs, as the Scots fought to repel the Norwegians who had landed. On 2 October, Haakon himself came ashore to take charge, but the best he could do was to achieve an orderly retreat from the shore back to his ships, which then left the Clyde and began the long voyage home.

The Pencil at Largs commemorates the Battle of Largs in 1263. *(Photo: Gordon Wright)*

The Bishop's Palace, Kirkwall, Orkney. *(Photo: Gordon Wright)*

The Battle of Largs marked the end of the old Norwegian domination of the western seaboard of Scotland, not because the battle itself was of any major importance, but because Haakon had been unable to arouse genuine support among the islanders. They had long followed Norway's lead and many families were more than half-Norse in their ancestry and traditions; but, as the generations had passed the geographical realities had come to affect man's thoughts and feelings. MacDonalds, Macruaries and MacSweens were now half-hearted at best in their loyalties to Norway, and the notion that their future interests lay in association with Scotland was clearly gaining ground.

So, the great king withdrew homewards. Depressed and ailing he rested in Orkney, where in the Bishop's Palace in Kirkwall, he died.

The new Norwegian king, Magnus, accepted that Norway's day of supremacy was over, and at Perth in 1266 a treaty gave to the Scottish king all Norwegian territories on the Scottish mainland and throughout the Western Isles. With this treaty, honourably observed by both sides, relations changed and friendship grew where previously enmity had been normal. In 1281 Alexander's daughter, Margaret, married King Eric, Haakon's grandson, and the relationship between Scotland and Norway was clearly intended to remain close.

With his other powerful neighbour, England, Alexander had maintained reasonably good relations, as long as Henry III reigned. That shifty monarch, having made his early attempts to bring Alexander and his kingdom under English feudal domination, seems to have abandoned such schemes, contenting himself by treating Alexander—who was, after all, his son-in-law—with apparently genuine personal affection; and when he was faced with baronial rebellion, the Scottish court was clearly sympathetic to Henry. But things were to change. In 1272 Henry died, and his son Edward became king. Then, in 1275, Margaret of England, Alexander's wife, also died, and Alexander was now dealing not with a reasonably genial father-in-law, but with his ex-brother-in-law, Edward I who was a very different man from his father and who had his own ideas for the future of Scotland.

It was therefore with some concern that Alexander and his courtiers travelled to England in 1278, to do homage for his English lands. The old images of kneeling Scottish kings haunted English minds. Alexander as a boy had avoided the trap set for him by Henry III. Would the new English king make some similar attempt?

When the meeting took place Edward and his ministers clearly meant mischief. Alexander swore to 'bear faith to Edward .... and will faithfully perform the services due for the lands I hold of him'. In that, all versions of events agree. But the Scottish records of the meeting state that Alexander added 'reserving my kingdom'. At this the Bishop of Norwich is reported to have suggested that the English king may claim the right to homage for that kingdom as well, to which Alexander responded 'No one has the right to homage for my kingdom, for I hold it of God alone'. The Scottish version may be doctored; the English version shows signs that *it* definitely was. However, there can be no doubt that Edward had tried to reassert the English claim that Scotland was merely a sub-kingdom, and, equally, no doubt that Alexander had rejected any idea of acceptance of the English case.

By 1280, then, Alexander might well be seen as the most successful of Scottish rulers. Scotland's territory was not so extensive as it had been briefly, under David I, but it was compact and stable. Scotland politically and Scotland geographically, coincided sensibly. The long contest with Norway was over. Relations with England were peaceable and courteous. Trade flourished, the land prospered, and good order prevailed at home. The future, too, looked bright. Alexander had two sons, both now grown men, and a daughter, queen by marriage of Norway. There seemed every reason to feel that Alexander's legacy of success would pass safely onwards through the generations.

Then, in 1281, David, the second son, died; in 1283 Margaret died also, leaving an infant daughter with the widower King Eric. Suddenly tragedy had struck Alexander's family, and danger approached his kingdom. In 1284 the heir to the throne, Alexander, also died; and the immediate future for Scotland was a matter of concern. Still, the Scottish state which

Alexander had fashioned held firm. The Scottish parliament in February confirmed the baby girl over in Norway as the legal heir to her grandfather, showing a degree of responsibility and discipline which testifies to the order and form which Alexander had given to his kingdom. However, one heir only, and that a female child, was not enough to give reassurance for future stability. Alexander, still only in early middle age, must marry again, and build a second family to guarantee the future. So, in November 1285 at Jedburgh, Alexander married Yolande of Dreux, thereby linking himself in friendship with powerful French interests.

On 18 March 1286, Alexander held council in Edinburgh, and, the business over, set off to cross into Fife to join Yolande at Kinghorn. The late afternoon and evening were dark and stormy, and the king was urged to stay in Edinburgh and wait for better conditions in the morning, but brushing aside all such advice the king left for the crossing of the River Forth at Queensferry. The ferry master there added his warning that the weather conditions made the crossing too dangerous to be prudently attempted, but even his professional advice could not deter Alexander from his purpose. He teased the ferryman, asking if he was afraid to die in his king's company, and under this kind of moral blackmail the ferryman gave way, prepared as he said, 'to meet my fate in company with your father's son'. The eight-oared ferry made slow progress in the teeth of the northerly gale, but eventually reached safety on the northern shore.

By now it was dark, and in the darkness and the gale, the master of the salt-works at Inverkeithing, who had come to meet the king, now argued with his master that he ought to remain in Inverkeithing till daylight. Having come through the dangers of the voyage Alexander saw no reason to fear the mere fact of darkness. He did ask for, and received, two local men to guide him and his three attendants on the last leg of his journey eastwards to Kinghorn.

As the king rode off into the darkness, Earl Patrick of Dunbar was chatting in his castle with a local worthy, Thomas of Ercildoune—'Thomas the Rhymer'—popularly believed to have the second-sight, and thus the power of prophecy. What would tomorrow bring, asked Patrick. 'Before the hour of noon there will assuredly be felt such a mighty storm in Scotland that its like has not been known for long ages past. The blast of it will cause nations to tremble, will make those who hear it dumb, will humble the high, and lay the strong level with the ground.' However impressed or alarmed Patrick may have been, Thomas's fears seemed absurd when the morning of the 19th dawned fair and grew fairer as the sun climbed higher. Just before noon, as Patrick was preparing for his midday meal, a messenger, urgent and desperate for audience with the earl, brought news that his king lay dead on the shore at Kinghorn.

His journey in the gathering darkness had led Alexander to a point where his horse lost its footing, whether on a cliff pathway, or in soft and treacherous sand on the shore, is not clear. By whatever accident the king was thrown, and died with his neck broken in his fall.

So Thomas's storm broke. The King was dead. His wife and his son's wife were childless. His children were gone, and only the girl Margaret, now the girl-queen of Scots, remained of the line which ran back through Malcolm Canmore to Kenneth MacAlpin.

In those circumstances Scotland's institutions and political leaders were going to be tested to the uttermost. Some institutions and some leaders stood the test, some only for a time, some for longer, but Scotland could never now be what Alexander and a secure monarchy might have made her. Not only would things never be the same; they would never again even be comparable. The steady, solid development which saw its peak in Alexander's reign was halted, and was never effectively resumed.

Scotland's luck died with Alexander at Kinghorn and never the slightest whiff of good fortune was to come the way of the Scottish people for the next seven centuries.

It was not long before people knew what they had lost; and the chronicler and historian recording these days, saw and felt the emotions of 1286 and the years which followed.

When Alexander our king was dead
That Scotland led in love and le
Away was sons of ale and bread
Of wine and wax, of gamyn and glee:
Our gold was turned into lead.
Christ, born into virginity,
Succour Scotland and remede
That stad is in perplexity.

le = law; sons = plenty; gamyn = pleasure.

Annual commemorative ceremony at the monument to King Alexander III at Kinghorn, 18 March 1990. *(Photo: Gordon Wright)*

Saving a Nation

The accession of the girl-queen, Margaret of Norway, put Scottish political stability to a severe test, but the work of David I and Alexander III proved equal to that test.

A six-man committee was appointed to act as Guardians of the Kingdom until such time as Margaret could take full responsibilities, and the immediate crisis did not seem to bring about any panic. She would grow, after all, and as long as her people remained loyal the crisis would pass. However, the Scottish leaders sought support in this dangerous moment from someone whose advice they valued and respected. Edward I of England was Margaret's great-uncle, and might well be seen by others, as well as by himself, as head of the family. Who was better able to bring support and reassurance to the Scots? Edward showed himself most willing to take charge of the situation, and now came forward with a most helpful plan. His son and the Scottish queen, though both were children, should marry, and with this new bond uniting the families and countries, he and the Guardians would guide Scotland safely through this crisis, towards days of harmony and closer unity.

This plan was approved at a conference of representatives from Scotland, England and Norway, and in July 1290 at Birgham on the Tweed a marriage treaty was agreed, and arrangements set on foot for the journey of Margaret from Norway to her waiting kingdom and her husband-to-be. Then came the final act of the tragedy which began with Alexander's fatal fall, as, by October 1290, 'there sounded through the people a sorrowful rumour that our Lady should be dead, on which account the kingdom of Scotland is disturbed and the community distracted'. They were right to be so disturbed and so distracted, as with the death of Margaret in the Orkney Islands there died the main line of the Scottish royal family. The succession now was a matter of controversy, and civil war was a very real possibility.

But even this crisis might be overcome if the Scots could arrange for arbitration instead of conflict. An arbiter would most desirably have close and sympathetic acquaintance with the Scots in their difficulties. He should have legal skill, and he should be able to enforce his decision. How fortunate the Scots were to have the very man available. King Edward was the late queen's great-uncle as well as her bereaved potential father-in-law. The Scots had already turned to him for advice, and would obviously do so again. He was also renowned for his legal skills which had earned for him the approving title of 'the English Justinian'. And he was most certainly powerful enough to enforce his decisions.

Thus it was agreed that claimants to the Scottish throne would present their various cases to Edward, and Edward would make the selection. Unfortunately Edward was not prepared to deal with the immediate problem on its own, but chose instead to turn first to the question of overlordship. Before he would proceed further he required from the Guardians, and from the claimants, their agreement that he was arbiter because he was overlord. He gave them three weeks to accept his demand, pointing out that if they persevered in their notion of independence they were perfectly entitled to defend that notion by force of arms. In this way Edward brought forward for immediate decision, all the old overlordship disputes. He had come so near to achieving his objectives in the Treaty of Birgham, that he was not going to allow the death of Margaret to frustrate him now.

The various claimants with greedy haste, and the other political leaders rather more slowly, accepted his demands and the process of selection began. He had thirteen major claimants to consider, but ten of them, for various reasons, were quickly and easily disposed of, and his choice was to lie with one or other of the three claimants descended from David, Earl of Huntingdon, the youngest son of David I. Earl David had three daughters, all of whom had male descendants. The question was, should the descendants of the eldest daughter take precedence over the descendants of her younger sisters? Today, the answer would be 'yes' but in 1291-92 there was not the same acceptance of the idea that any precedence existed among daughters.

There was the added complication that the descendant of the eldest daughter was Earl David's great-grandson, while the descendant of the second daughter was his grandson, and therefore closer in blood to the common ancestor.

After much examination of precedents elsewhere in the feudal world it was decided that seniority was to be preferred to 'nearness in blood', and the Scottish crown was therefore awarded to Earl David's great-grandson, John Balliol, to the keen disappointment of Earl David's grandson, Robert Bruce, who had once, in the days of Alexander II, been designated heir, but who now in old age, saw all ambition ended.

John Balliol's accession was marred by the bullying approach employed by Edward, and his early experience as King of Scots was rendered unhappy by further bullying. Anxious, no doubt, to make his point clear, Edward required various displays of obedience from Balliol, for whom humiliation at Edward's hands seemed likely to become a way of life.

But even such a shrewd man as Edward was capable of misjudgement, and even Balliol could be provoked beyond endurance. That provocation came when, in 1295, Edward was about to mount an expedition against France and ordered Balliol, as his feudal inferior, to join him in the war which was about to commence. The worm now turned. Balliol, known to his derisive subjects as 'Toom Tabard'—'empty coat' or 'stuffed shirt'—had some pride, and some awareness that nothing but exploitation and humiliation faced him in the future. Accordingly, instead of obeying, he renounced his allegiance to Edward, and instead entered into an alliance with France, whereby the two countries agreed to take joint military action against England whenever the latter attacked either of them. This Franco-Scottish alliance—the Auld Alliance—was to be the basis of Scottish foreign policy for almost 300 years.

Edward's punishment of Balliol's defiance was swift and savage. In 1296 English forces invaded Scotland. Berwick was besieged, stormed and destroyed, its people massacred and its prosperity gone for ever. Balliol's army was shattered in battle at Dunbar, and by the late summer his reign was over. On 2 July he surrendered to Edward 'the land of Scotland and all its people', and he made his own personal and symbolic act of submission, barefoot, half-naked and unarmed, in the church of Stracathro.

Well pleased with himself, Edward had a brisk look around his new property, and returned home. There was to be no new puppet king. Robert Bruce ventured to suggest that this might be his hour, drawing from Edward the contemptuous response that he had better things to do than go round conquering kingdoms for Bruce. Instead he placed control of Scotland in the hands of English officials; John de Warenne, Earl of Surrey, was military commander, and Hugh de Cressingham, churchman and bureaucrat, was responsible for civil administration. The absorption of Scotland into Edward's Greater England, seemed now inevitable, and even the records of government and the symbols of nationhood were removed to England, the fragment of the True Cross from Holyrood and the Stone of Destiny from Scone. As for resistance, none was to be anticipated, as the landowners of Scotland hurriedly and tactfully rushed to place their names on a list of those doing homage to Edward—a list which later generations were to know, derisively, as 'the Ragman's Roll'.

And yet resistance there was—a heroic episode which became the great national myth or folk-memory of Scotland. Some guerrilla activity was undertaken by Sir William Douglas in the south and by Andrew de Moray in the north, but most famous and honoured of all these resistance leaders was William Wallace. Countless words have been written about Wallace, most of them based upon the epic poem *The Wallace*, written by Henry the Minstrel or 'Blind Harry', some two centuries after the events which he describes. Yet Harry's narrative, where it can be checked against the references to Wallace which are to be found in the chronicles of his time, stands up to scrutiny rather well. The probability must be that Harry was working from an oral tradition, which must indicate that Wallace was a subject of hero-worship and legend for many generations before Harry wrote his poem.

The story is now widely familiar and widely available. Its hero is the younger son of a knight who held lands as a tenant of the Stewards at Elderslie in Renfrewshire. Born around 1270 he was approaching manhood as the disasters following Alexander's death were occurring. Taught by an uncle, a priest at Dunipace, to cherish the idea of freedom, his education was carried forward at the church school in Dundee. His presence in the east of the country is accounted for by the tradition that his father had become politically unpopular through his active opposition to the growing English domination which followed the Treaty of Birgham, and the young Wallace with his mother moved discreetly to live with relatives in the Carse of Gowrie. In Dundee an adolescent dispute ended with Wallace killing the son of the commander of Dundee's English garrison, for which deed he

41

The Wallace Monument at Bemersyde near Dryburgh. *(Photo: Gordon Wright)*

became—and, in English eyes, remained—an outlaw.

If an outlaw he was, he seems to have felt that he might as well act the part; and from 1292 he is found making trouble for the English authorities in widely-scattered parts of the country. It is possible that he fought in Balliol's army at Dunbar in 1296; and certainly in 1297, he emerged as the sharpest thorn in English flesh. His travels in 1297 brought him into repeated skirmishes with English forces over an area ranging from Loch Awe in the north to Lochmaben in the south. His father had by now fallen victim to English soldiers, and Wallace suffered the further tragedy of having his wife—actual or intended—killed by the English commander in Lanark, because she had assisted him to escape from an English force which had come near to capturing him. To his nationalist motives there was now added the incentive of personal revenge, and the killer of Marion Braidfute fell victim to Wallace's rage and grief.

He was capable of taking vengeance for others as well. When the English governor of Ayr invited local Scottish leaders to meet him and then had them all hanged as they arrived, Wallace responded by taking his men into Ayr, securing the doors of the buildings where English soldiers lay, and setting fire to them. There is a local tradition that the Scots watched Ayr burn from a hilltop near Tarbolton a few miles from the stricken town.

By now Wallace was no mere outlaw; he was intolerable to King Edward and his officials in Scotland who mounted a full-scale military operation to destroy him. He was engaged in besieging the castle of Dundee when reports came to him of English preparations to cross the Forth to seek and destroy 'this robber' as the English chroniclers dubbed him. Leaving the siege to his local supporters, Wallace made for the only route north which an English army could take—the crossing of the Forth at Stirling. There he positioned his men on the north bank of the river, and awaited the English attack.

Argument on tactics raged briefly in the English camp. Surrey, who knew more than most about battles, had no wish to direct his army across the narrow bridge, preferring to delay matters, and make a crossing over a ford a short distance upstream. His civilian colleague, Cressingham, whose duties included providing for payment of the costs of the campaign, preferred a quick strike, and strutted off across the bridge. Wallace held his men back until he felt that the English force which had reached the northern bank was as large as his army could handle; then he had a small Scottish force seize the northern end of the bridge while the bulk of his army set about the destruction of the English who had crossed. The result was a total defeat for Edward's army of occupation. Cressingham was killed, and the Scots made souvenirs of his skin. Surrey fled with the remains of his army to Berwick, and Wallace and his men were now the only power in Scotland. Wallace himself was left in sole command (his ally, Andrew de Moray, having died of wounds received in the battle), and, as though to bring some show of normality into the administration of the country, he now took the title of 'Guardian of Scotland', acting in the name of King John.

The amazing thing about his success, apart from his obviously remarkable talents as a fighting leader, was that this man had no aristocratic

43

Battle of Stirling Bridge

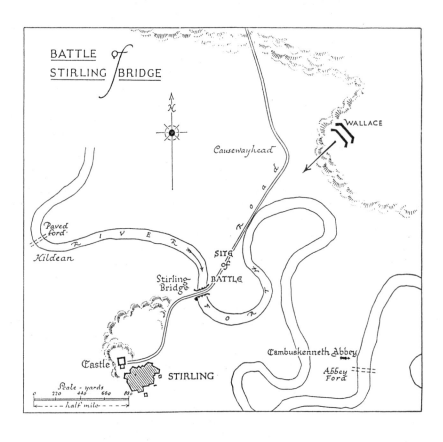

advantages. He was not born into leadership or into statecraft, but had earned leadership and honour by his courage, his skill and his devotion to his country. Wallace's career proves beyond argument that Scotland was now more than a mere theory or legal concept, but was a nation in the minds and hearts of its people—which is what really matters.

But his modest social status did present problems. It would never be easy for the nobility to endure leadership even of a proven patriot and warrior indefinitely. Some were jealous no doubt; most had played no part whatever in the national struggle, and some who had, like the young Robert Bruce of Annandale and Carrick, could not be expected to follow the lead of a leader who acted in the name of John Balliol. The probability had to be that Wallace's tenure of power and influence would be purely temporary.

He made what use he could of his time as Guardian, seeking to restore normality in trade and diplomacy, trying to persuade the rulers of Europe to accept that Scotland was once more a free participant in world affairs. Most were perfectly civil, and may even have been sympathetic, but all would know that Edward was not the man to let matters rest.

In 1298 Edward led his army—enormous by the standards of the time— into Scotland to punish this bandit, this terrorist, who had so defied and humiliated him. Against such power as Edward's, no Scottish force could reasonably hope for success in battle. The best hope, then and always, for the Scots, lay in retreat and delay; avoiding pitched battles, keeping an armed force in existence, while the English were drawn further from their bases into remoter parts until winter approached, supplies ran short and retreat became necessary. Wallace appears to have intended to follow such a strategy, but Edward was able to keep up such a hot pursuit that the Scottish army found itself forced to turn and fight at Falkirk.

Even then there was still hope. The Scottish schiltrons—densely assembled circles of spearmen—could be relied upon to beat back as many cavalry charges as an enemy cared to make, but unfortunately for the Scots Edward had a new military tactic at his disposal. Before he had found the opportunity to seize control of Scotland he had already conquered Wales, and his army at Falkirk had a large force of Welsh archers. These bowmen were able to inflict heavy losses upon the schiltrons from a safe distance, tearing gaps in the Scottish ranks through which English cavalry could in due course charge. The way to deal with archers was to send cavalry against them, and this Wallace tried to do. But cavalry—armoured knights—were drawn from the ranks of the nobility and the gentry, who alone could afford horses and armour. Here at last Wallace's lack of aristocratic support proved crucial. The small cavalry force which he did have, saw itself overmatched, considered the likely outcome of the battle, and ran away. The Scottish formation was gradually broken down, and was soon retreating into the safety of the Torwood, which Wallace had perhaps seen as a refuge if things went badly.

With his defeat, his power was gone. He resigned his position as Guardian, being replaced by the leaders of the two main political factions in Scotland—John Comyn and Robert Bruce, together with Bishop Lamberton of St. Andrews. Wallace continued, it seems, to conduct some

45

guerrilla operations, which were still possible, because he had come so near to success. Only a few weeks after his victory, Edward had had to lead his hungry army back home, leaving Scotland far from properly under control. Also, Wallace seems to have gone on diplomatic missions seeking moral support in Norway, in France and, perhaps, in Rome.

It is said that Edward tried to win Wallace over, offering perhaps even the crown itself, if only he would agree to hold it as Edward's subordinate. No temptations worked; Wallace remained irreconcilable, and English pride and security alike required his destruction.

Comyn and Bruce, and various lesser persons, were all at one time or another bidden by Edward to secure and hand over Wallace to him. How hard they tried, we do not know, but for a man hunted as Wallace now was, there must always be the danger of betrayal.

On 5 August 1305, Wallace and two followers settled for the night in the house of Ralph Rae at Robroyston. During the night, we are told, one of Wallace's companions, a relative of Sir John Stewart of Menteith (who in his time had held Dumbarton Castle for both the Scots and the English), betrayed Wallace and opened the door to Menteith's men. Their story at first was that, in the interests of peace, Wallace was to go to be in Menteith's charge at Dumbarton, but once subdued, he was instead handed over to an English escort, and hurried to London. Menteith's reward was £151.

On 23 August in Westminster Hall Edward at last confronted this man who had refused all attempts to win him over, or to make him abandon his loyalty to his own independent country. He was an outlaw in English eyes, and, as such, received no trial, but simply a statement of his offences and the sentence which they incurred. Edward personally had devised the English penalty for treason. Wallace was slowly tortured to death and his head displayed on Tower Bridge. His limbs were exhibited at Newcastle, Berwick, Stirling and Perth as a warning to others. The English Justinian, and probably England's greatest King, was also a demented sadist it would seem.

So Wallace died, his bravery and his defiance maintained to the end. His heroism and his total selflessness have earned for him the unforgetting reverence of his people. Only one other Scot has become a national myth, and he—Robert Burns—was moved in all his opinions by the story and the memory of Wallace. 'The story of Wallace' Burns wrote, 'poured a tide of Scottish prejudice into my veins, which will boil along there till the floodgates of life shut in eternal rest'. Millions of Scots down through the centuries have experienced exactly the same emotion.

Scottish resistance after Wallace's defeat did continue and some modest local successes were recorded, but there was no real prospect that the Comyns and Bruce would for long be able to co-operate. John Comyn, head of the family since his father's death in 1303, was Balliol's nephew, his supporter and possibly his successor, assuming that King John would never venture to return from his exile. Bruce on the other hand, was rival to both Balliol and Comyn. The co-operation between them ended with Bruce's resignation of his position as joint Guardian. Comyn and other leaders continued to offer defiance to England, but this resistance crumbled when

Edward himself reappeared in Scotland, and compelled the submission of all the Scots leaders in February 1304. Only Stirling Castle held out longer and its Governor, Oliphant, surrendered in July. With these surrenders, and the capture of Wallace in the following year, Scotland once again must have seemed subdued beyond all hope of recovery.

What Bruce did during those years remains a matter for controversy. Entering into Edward's peace, he was from time to time shown marks of the English king's approval and favour. Yet, given his pedigree and the ambitions of his family for which he was now responsible, it was unlikely that Bruce any more than Comyn, would accept English conquest and the permanent extinction of the Scottish monarchy. Just what intrigues these men and their various supporters were up to will never be known, but, for whatever purpose, they met by arrangement on 10 February 1306, in Greyfriars Church, Dumfries.

The generally accepted view is that they had already been plotting to take joint action against Edward, and that Comyn had, deliberately or otherwise, allowed this to become known. Certainly Bruce had left London in great haste some weeks earlier (warned, according to legend, by the Earl of Gloucester), and he is thought to have come to suspect Comyn of treachery. At all events, the two met and quarrelled, and Bruce stabbed Comyn close by the very altar of the church. The murder was then completed by some of Bruce's associates, and Bruce was now in a desperate position. The murder had turned the political rivalry of two families into a blood feud. The location of the deed made him guilty of sacrilege in the eyes of the Church, from which he was in due course excommunicated. And when people, among them King Edward, began to ask themselves just why the meeting had taken place, and why Bruce had struck down Comyn, they were bound to assume that some sort of conspiracy was afoot. For Bruce to submit to legal process for the murder was inviting the end of all his hopes, and perhaps his life. To attempt to offer any explanation to a suspicious Edward was no more attractive a task. In the circumstances, making the best of a bad job, his wisest course might be openly to claim the crown, and call for support.

His first act was to make contact with his old family ally, Bishop Wishart of Glasgow, who proved remarkably unconcerned about sacrilege and perfectly ready to back Bruce in his pursuit of the throne. On Palm Sunday, 27 March 1307, Wishart and Lamberton supervised the crowning of Bruce as King of Scots at Scone.

Of his adventures thereafter, there is a wealth of information. English and Scottish chronicles give much more information about Bruce than they ever did about Wallace. Bruce had so many advantages that Wallace never could hope for. He was of royal blood, and now king; he had many powerful friends, and he was fighting in his own name to maintain his new dignity. Where the chronicles are silent, the story of Bruce can be picked up in the epic poem *The Brus*, by John Barbour, who did for Bruce what Blind Harry did for Wallace.

From these sources we learn of Bruce's desperate struggle in the early

47

years of his kingship. Surprised and defeated by an English force at Methven in Perthshire in 1307; coming close to death in a skirmish with the Macdougalls of Lorne, relatives and supporters of the Balliol/Comyn cause; a fugitive, reduced to a mere handful of followers, tracked by hunting dogs, and a fugitive again, driven into exile on some remote island, where close to despair, he is reputed to have learned determination from the labours of a spider.

But gradually the tide turned, and supporters rallied to him. His best piece of good fortune was the death in 1307 of the great King Edward, who died on the way north yet again to deal with this latest piece of Scottish disobedience. Bruce's supporters proved to be men of some military skill, showing especial talents in capturing castles from their English garrisons. Thomas Randolph captured Edinburgh, after a hair-raising climb up the Castle rock. James Douglas made himself especially feared by the English as he waged ruthless war in his own family lands in the Border country. Even humble men like the Linlithgow farmer, Binning, showed great ingenuity, jamming a cart between the drawbridge and portcullis of Linlithgow Castle, opening the way for Scots to break in and overpower the garrison. The campaign to win back castles went on relentlessly. When a castle was captured it was 'slighted', its foundations undermined and one or more of its walls collapsed. There was no attempt to place Scottish garrisons in the castles. If Bruce had followed that plan he would merely have spread his forces thinly about the country, to be picked off one by one by English counter attacks. The castles were rendered useless, depriving the English of their strong points, their armouries, and their stores. By 1314 only two major castles—Bothwell and Stirling—remained in English hands.

Stirling had been besieged by a Scottish force under King Robert's brother Edward. Edward was an impatient soul, who fretted at the long drawn out siege. His patience ebbing fast, he and the English governor, Philip Mowbray, agreed to bring matters to a head by a kind of challenge. Mowbray agreed that if Stirling was not relieved by an English force by midsummer 1314, he would surrender. By this bargain Mowbray left his king, Edward II, no choice but to try to break the Scottish siege; and Edward Bruce left his brother no choice but to confront the English army which must now appear. Such a pitched battle was what King Robert had sought to avoid; the fate of Wallace's army at Falkirk did not encourage any such course of action, but there was no escape now.

The English army—greater than any ever before mustered against Scotland—made its way north, starting from its assembly point at Wark on 10 June. By 21 June Edward was in Edinburgh, planning to be in Stirling by the 23 June.

Bruce had spent the spring and early summer preparing his ground and drilling his men. His army, organised in three divisions with a reserve behind them, lay across the road which led into Stirling from the south. There were no natural obstacles to place between the Scots and charging English cavalry, so artificial obstacles had to be provided. Metal spikes or 'calthrops' which would lame horses, were scattered along the Scottish

Battle of Bannockburn

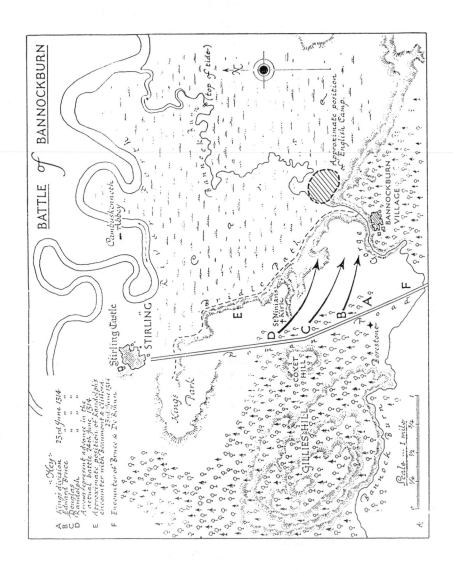

front; and pits were dug which, it was hoped, would serve as traps for the attackers.

By late afternoon on 23 June, the armies were in contact, and it became evident that Edward and his generals intended to waste no time. Sir Henry de Bohun, correctly identifying as King Robert the Scottish officer who was moving back and forth along his lines, decided that matters could be settled quickly, and charged at full gallop upon his intended victim. At the last possible moment Bruce turned his horse aside, and as de Bohun went thundering past, brought his axe down upon the knight's head, leaving him lifeless before the astonished gaze of both armies.

First blood to the Scots, but more discouragement awaited the English. An attempt to outflank Randolph's division on the Scots' left was beaten back in a skirmish around St. Ninian's church, and as darkness fell there was doubt and anxiety in the English camp. Edward and his generals had seen fit to move their men to their right, eastward, on to the low-lying ground through which flowed the Bannockburn. The result of this manoeuvre was that Bruce's prepared defences were now useless. The English charge would come not from the south, but from the east. Bruce had to reorganise his men in some haste, and as dawn broke the Scots were ready, looking down the slope at the mighty force which they would shortly have to face.

At some stage during the night, Bruce had revised his plans. Deprived of his static defences he may have been considering retreat, losing thereby the opportunity of gaining Stirling castle, but saving his army to fight in more favourable surroundings. But there had come to the Scottish camp Sir Alexander Seton, a Scot who had been in the English army, presumably as a Balliol partisan, but who had now either repented, or had detected a change in the winds of war. Seton brought Bruce news of an English army, worried and ill-at-ease, vulnerable to any attack which the Scots might care to mount. It may be that this advice lay behind the decision which Bruce now took. Not only would he fight, but he would not have his men stand passively in their schiltrons to await the English attack. On the contrary, he would take the initiative, and move upon the English who would not be anticipating this mobility from the Scots.

So, as the English soldiers began to make their preparations they were astonished to see the Scottish divisions on the slopes above them begin to march down upon them. As one chronicler says, 'the English army .... mounted in great alarm'. For a brief moment their alarm may have subsided, as the Scottish force was suddenly seen to kneel, while along their ranks rode the Abbot of Inchaffray, leading the Scots in the Lord's Prayer, and granting them absolution. Edward himself misunderstood the meaning of the scene. The Scots, he suggested, were kneeling for mercy from him, their aggrieved overlord. Another Balliol Scot, watching beside Edward, put him right. The Scots he pointed out, many of them on the point of death, were asking for God's mercy, not his.

Bruce, so Barbour tells us, spoke briefly to encourage his men. He would know that all the painfully won gains of the past eight years could now be lost in a matter of minutes; and he and his supporters must also have known that if Bruce failed here, there was no one else to whom Scotland could look

Monument to King Robert the Bruce at Bannockburn. *(Photo: Gordon Wright)*

for leadership and victory. It had become, as Burns was later to put it, a matter of do or die.

The various chroniclers do their best to explain what then happened. The advancing Scots were subjected to volleys from the English—or Welsh—archers, who were in turn counter-attacked by the Scottish horse, whose absence had doomed Wallace at Falkirk. So, the archers fell back, and the English cavalry moved through to take up the attack. 'The great horses of the English charged the pikes of the Scots as it were into a dense forest .... and so they remained without movement for a while.' In that sentence lies the key to an understanding of the battle. The field, from the English point of view, was over-crowded. By their manoeuvre of the 23rd, they had turned the Scottish flank, but in doing so they had placed themselves on a restricted arena, with marshes and streams to their right and their rear; and, to their left, a short but fairly deep gorge through which flowed the Bannock burn. There was no way out, except uphill through the Scottish ranks; and as the Scots pressed forward, and the English archers struggled among the English cavalry, and the English foot were pushed forward to play their part, the English found themselves in such a tangle that their cavalry leaders sought to give ground and regroup for a fresh attack.

But they had no ground to give. 'They were jammed together and could not operate against them, so direfully were their horses impaled on the pikes.' The troops in the English rear fell back upon the ditch of Bannockburn, tumbling one over the other. 'Many nobles and others fell into it with their horses in the crush .... never able to extricate themselves from the ditch.'

The true victor of Bannockburn in a sense, therefore, was the battle-field. Marshes and streams claimed armoured men, unable to rise if they fell. The gorge, we are told, was so filled with the bodies of men and horses that it was possible to walk across it from one bank to the other as though on level ground. From this horror the English army now broke and fled. Edward himself escaped around the Scots' left, and made for Stirling Castle. Mowbray reminded his king that he would be handing the castle over to the Scots in accordance with his bargain with Edward Bruce, and so the hapless king had to circle the battlefield once more, seeking an escape route which would bring him to Dunbar and ships which would take him back to England and safety.

An English rearguard fought on, their last shreds of confidence destroyed by the appearance from the Gillies Hill of what seemed to them a new Scottish army. The old-fashioned view was that this force was 'the camp-followers', little more than vultures come to pick up whatever spoils could be got from the dead and wounded of the defeated army. In more modern times the favoured explanation has been that these 'small folk' were a kind of enthusiastic but only half-armed reserve, commendably anxious to play their part in the victory. The English were probably beaten anyway, but it is reasonable to assume that any lingering confidence would vanish as what seemed to be Scottish reinforcements appeared

Most remaining English forces clustered around the castle rock, and there surrendered. They may well have saved their king and many of their escaping leaders, because, with such a large force to guard, Bruce could never allow his own army to break up in pursuit of the fugitives.

Edward's escape meant that Bannockburn was not as decisive as it might have been, but for the moment the Scottish victory was total. Bothwell Castle was abandoned, and the remnants of the English army fled back to Carlisle, where the monks of Lanercost Priory were first to hear of the disaster, and the horrors of that dreadful gorge.

Bruce was now king beyond dispute and Scotland had, under him, maintained its independence by force of arms, as Edward I had sarcastically suggested they might feel free to try, those many years ago at Birgham. But the war did not end, because the English acceptance of defeat was not offered. Each year brought Scottish armies raiding into the north of England, and Edward Bruce even contrived to attack the English in Ireland, and to make himself briefly king of that country.

In their desire for peace and acknowledgement of their independence, the Scots turned for help to the best international authority available—the Pope, whose wish, they suggested, ought to be to see peace among Christian peoples. Popes, however, were usually political partisans, and the Papacy in the years after Bannockburn was pro-English. The Scots persevered with

The Declaration of Arbroath, 1320. *(From the original in the Scottish Record Office)*

diplomacy and with propaganda, and in 1320 produced a document which had characteristics of both.

The Scottish church had been steadfastly nationalist all through the years since 1286. Bishops Wishart and Lamberton were proven patriots, but others too deserve to be similarly remembered. Churchmen were after all, the literate class in medieval society, and Scottish churchmen had undertaken the task of expounding and justifying the Scottish case for independence. In 1320, meeting at Arbroath Abbey, the leaders of the community of Scotland put their seals to a document prepared, almost certainly, by Bernard de Linton, abbot and civil servant, which yet again, but more fully now than ever before, spelled out Scotland's claim to identity and independence.

Scotland, they reminded Pope John, to whom the Declaration was addressed, had been a kingdom when England was big enough for seven kings. They had endured attack from King Edward who had taken advantage of their misfortunes and had worked to destroy their freedom under guise of friendship. Fate had given them as leader and deliverer, King Robert. Yet—and this is the remarkable passage—'if he should abandon our cause .... we should make every endeavour to expel him as our enemy and the subverter of his rights and ours, and choose another for our king'. There are those who look for the origins of monarchy dependent upon popular will, in the writing of seventeenth century English philosophers. Very clearly the Scots had stumbled upon the concept of conditional monarchy several centuries earlier.

Finally, in case Pope John or his cardinals thought that Scottish resistance to English ambitions was merely a passing fad, de Linton offered to his countrymen for their approval a pledge of determination free of all ambiguity. 'For so long as a hundred of us shall remain alive we shall never accept subjection to the domination of the English. For we fight not for glory, or riches or honour, but for freedom alone which no good man will consent to lose but with his life.'

And yet the Pope remained full of complaint and censure, the English would not concede independence, and the war dragged on. Not until political crisis in England had brought about the deposition and murder of Edward II did the English parliament weary of paying the bills for endless warfare, and force peace upon their boy king Edward III and his advisers. So, in 1328 the English parliament meeting at Northampton agreed to terms of peace. Bruce was at last addressed with all terms of respect due to an independent monarch, and the English claims to overlordship were renounced.

Bruce's heir, the four-year-old David, son of King Robert's second marriage, was married to Joan of England, the six-year-old sister of Edward III. It was almost as though the kingdoms were as they had been when King Edward had arranged the future at Birgham. In the years which lay between, Edward had earned and gloried in the title 'Hammer of the Scots', but his hammer blows had moulded and tempered the Scottish nation. The long wars fought to maintain independence had removed, for the moment, any doubt that independence was something to be regarded as normal.

The Days of James IV

The story of events in Scotland in the two centuries or so which followed the Treaty of Northampton makes depressing reading. Ill-wishers are given ample reason to sneer or to deride, and Scots themselves may well feel that the conduct of their countrymen during those generations justifies the national inferiority complex.

The events are melodramatic. Two kings murdered; two killed on the battlefield; an heir to the throne thought to have been murdered by his wicked uncle; two kings made prisoners of war, and subsequently ransomed; noblemen turning to treason, and kings stooping to judicial murder; kings kidnapped and used as instruments in the schemes of greedy and ambitious politicians—with such a tale of horror and catastrophe it is not surprising that while specialist students of the period may understand many of the issues, the general observer is likely to be left with a confused and irritating picture of the times.

Many things which happened were disgraceful and even more were pitiful, but there were reasons for them all. For instance, at this stage of political sophistication, the personality and capacities of the king were of the greatest importance in determining whether the country would prosper or decline. Of the eight kings who followed Robert Bruce who died in 1329, only two were adults, and both had their limitations. David II was five; James I was twelve; James II was six; James III was ten; James IV was fifteen and James V one year and a few months old. At regular intervals, therefore, the Scots endured lengthy royal minorities, and the consequent need to find suitable regents or Guardians. In such circumstances competition for power, and the formation of political factions among the powerful, are all too probable.

Also, there were moments when the freakishness of the hereditary principle worked to the country's disadvantage. It was in retrospect for instance, rather a pity that Bruce had a second marriage and a male heir in the person of David II. If Thomas Randolph had been, not Guardian, but king, in 1329, things might have gone rather better than they did. Or again, if Robert II had been succeeded by his ablest son rather than his eldest, the nation would have been spared Robert III and the wretched experience of his rule.

So, recurring minorities brought rivalries, but rivalries were bequeathed to Scotland by Robert II. He had married twice, and fathered twenty-one children. Each son and each son's descendants carried ambitious feelings, and there lingered for several generations a potential for trouble, as the families deriving from his second marriage returned every so often to the assertion that his first marriage was unlawful and its heirs therefore illegitimate. For his many daughters Robert had to find husbands, and he

55

thus drew close to the royal family by marriage many families which might better have been kept at a safer distance.

In addition to this company of royal and semi-royal aspirants to power and place, there were also families whose ambitions sprang from their vast estates which conferred upon them great wealth in rentals and great strength in the number of their tenants who could be soldiers in their lord's interest. Two families in particular bedevilled the state—the Douglasses and the MacDonalds of the Isles. The Douglas power had honourable beginnings in the contribution of Bruce's great captain Sir James, and none would feel resentment or surprise that lands were bestowed upon the family whose head had so deserved the respect of his countrymen and the generosity of his king. But Sir James died soon after his master, carrying Bruce's heart into battle against the Saracens in Spain; and his successors, inheritors of great possessions, did not necessarily share his qualities. Through time the main line of the family—the 'Black' Douglases—became intolerable to the crown in their power and their arrogance and were crushed by murders, battle and eventually forfeiture of their lands. But a branch of the family—the 'Red' Douglases—became Earls of Angus, and long survived to make a nuisance of themselves.

The MacDonalds—especially those based in Islay—were the heirs of the semi-independent Lords of the Isles looking back to the great half-Norse half-Gaelic Somerled as their ancestor. The Lords of the Isles had ruled as virtual monarchs, and had prompted many Scottish kings to mount campaigns against them. The MacDougalls had lost their power through their backing of Balliol against Bruce, but the other line of Somerled's heirs, Clan Donald, remained proud and powerful.

There was, of course, one remaining menace to Scotland and her rulers—England. English recognition of Scottish independence had been grudging and totally insincere, and thus England's kings took every possible opportunity to benefit from Scotland's recurring misfortunes. They were able to inflict upon the Scots a succession of disastrous defeats, which the Scots were able to survive only because from the 1330's onwards, England became embroiled in the Hundred Years War with France, and later in the civil wars of the Roses. But defeats like Dupplin Moor in 1332, Halidon Hill in 1333, Neville's Cross in 1346 were fit to rank as Scottish disasters with Dunbar and Falkirk.

So, weakened by internal faction, which English kings fostered and used to the fullest possible extent, Scotland stumbled through the generations, never conquered, but constantly weakened, held together by some luck, occasional competence from her kings, and the commendable loyalty of some of the nobility.

The one moment upon which later generations could look back with any real pride was the brilliant reign of James IV which ended, in the best Scottish tradition, with the most heart-rending of national tragedies. No one could have foreseen that the boy of fifteen, who came to the throne as a result of a rebellion against his father, in which he himself had participated, would become the king of Scots most brilliant in the judgement of later generations. David I and Alexander III are, in comparison, rather shadowy figures, and Robert I's fame is bound up totally with the winning of independence. James's career we can study, from its beginning to its end, and he emerges from scrutiny as a man possessed of all the qualities which would ideally be found in a leader. As skilled an administrator as James I; as alert and lively of mind as James II, and as cultured as James III he had all the good points of his predecessors and showed none of their defects. He was free of the cruelty which demeaned James I; he lacked—until the very end of his life—the impulsiveness of James II, and he had the dignity and self assurance which his father so damagingly lacked.

Once old enough to devise his own priorities he moved to establish royal authority in the Highlands and Islands once and for all.

James, perhaps initially with seaborne trade in mind, had Parliament pass a Shipping Act, requiring all coastal burghs to build twenty ton ships in the national interest. Between then and 1506 James led several expeditions into the Hebrides, compelling the submission gradually of the MacDonalds and the lesser chiefs who had obeyed them. John of the Isles submitted in 1494, and ended his days as a monk in Paisley Abbey in 1498. The entire ruling family of Islay resisted unwisely and were captured and executed—father and four sons—in 1494. The last resistance ended in 1506, and Donald, last claimant to the 'Lord of the Isles' title, remained a prisoner in Edinburgh castle for almost forty years.

These expeditions had shown the importance of naval power, and revealed the good fortune which James enjoyed in having the services of famous and brilliant sea-captains like Sir Andrew Wood of Largo, and the

Sir Andrew Wood's Tower, Upper Largo, Fife. *(Photo: Gordon Wright)*

three Barton brothers, all of whom enjoyed a reputation extending throughout Western Europe. Building upon his success James arranged for the construction of what was virtually a Scottish Royal Navy, the flagship being the *Great Michael*, a giant among ships of its time. According to tradition all the oak trees in Fife were felled to provide for the *Great Michael's* building, and under the command of Sir Andrew Wood the fleet became for James a source of great pride and satisfaction.

In addition to naval power, James arranged for future control of the islands and the remoter west by building royal castles at Tarbert and Dunaverty; but most important of all, he delegated responsibility for the maintenance of order in the area, to lieutenants upon whom he was prepared to rely. He was not the first king to use such a method, but the consequences of James's plan were to endure into modern times.

His chosen instruments were the Earl of Huntly, head of the wide network of landowners of the Gordon family, whose power base was in the north-east; and the Earl of Argyle, head of an even more impressive array of Campbell chiefs in the west. The Huntly family had been traditionally royalist and loyal; the then Earl had given vital help to James II against Douglas allies in the 1450's, and in 1488 Huntly had fought for his king, James III at Sauchieburn. The loyalty of the Campbells went back even further to the days when Sir Neil Campbell of Lochawe chose to serve and follow Robert Bruce, and founded the family fortunes in so doing. So in the north-east and north, the Gordons acted for the crown; and in the west it was now the Campbell galleys and Campbell military power which was crucial.

The pacification of the Highlands and Islands complete, James imposed order similarly in the Borders, and good order for the future was to be guaranteed by a revised legal apparatus involving a more or less permanent Law Court in Edinburgh, and by regular tours of Justiciars in support of local sheriffs in areas judged to be in need of such supervision. James appears to have appreciated the advantages of involving a wider proportion of his subjects in public affairs, and he gave new importance to Parliament, requiring freeholders in the shires and merchants in the burghs to participate in selection of representatives and, if themselves selected, to undertake the obligations of parliamentary business.

Peace and order achieved, James sought to enhance the economic strength of his country. The long wars with England, though not destroying Scottish independence, had gravely injured the Scottish economy, as English invaders or retreating Scots burned and destroyed crops and property at times almost annually. It has been asserted that Scotland was economically stronger in the days of Alexander III than in the days of James III. Now James and his advisers acted to reform the currency, to impose standard measures of weight and volume, all to inspire greater confidence in Scottish commerce. An export trade was fostered with the establishment of a Scottish base, or 'staple', first at Middelburg and then at Veere (or 'Campveere') in the Netherlands.

Domestic efficiency and commercial improvement enhanced Scotland's influence abroad, and under James, Scotland came to enjoy diplomatic importance. Scottish support was given to, and welcomed by, Denmark under pressure from Swedish enemies; to Guelders, against the Hapsburgs of Austria, and, of course, to France, enemy of England and England's allies, Spain and Austria.

In his relations with England, James had been fortunate in having to deal with Henry VII, a ruler of the utmost shrewdness and the least possible emotion, whose utter realism led him to see that nothing useful was to be gained from stirring up trouble on his northern border; and his calm even survived James's romantic support for Perkin Warbeck who sought to overthrow Henry by claiming to be the rightful Yorkist king of England. Warbeck's failure ended James's lapse into folly, and entering into a truce with England, James it would seem, was beginning to question the value of the French alliance. A change in Scottish attitudes certainly seemed to be indicated by the marriage in 1503 of James and Margaret Tudor, daughter of Henry VII. Henry, an ever-patient man, was content to see this drawing closer of Scotland and England. To those in England who feared future Scottish influence, Henry offered the reassurance that 'the greater will draw the less.'

In 1509 the English crown passed to Henry VIII, the antithesis of his father—romantic, overbearing, and emotional, and a much more dangerous neighbour. Relations between England and Scotland rapidly deteriorated. English ships attacked Andrew Barton at sea, alleging piracy, and Henry was cold in his rejection of James's complaints. In 1512 Henry, with his Spanish and Austrian allies in the so-called Holy League, attacked France. James renewed the alliance with France, but seems to have hoped to mediate rather than fight. But skirmishing began along the Border; French defeats occurred, and the French queen, who knew her man, appealed to James's romantic and chivalrous streak, sending him her ring, and asking him to 'break a lance' in England for her sake.

This misguided vision of himself as a knight, upon whom damsels in distress might call for aid, was the fatal flaw in James's character. All his previous skill and experience were set aside, as his honour was now appealed to. He called his army to muster on the Burghmuir of Edinburgh and their response testifies to James's work in uniting his country. From all parts of his country, and from families often in past conflict with one another, they came to his summons.

With perhaps the largest Scottish army ever assembled James crossed the border, captured key English strongholds and awaited the oncoming English army under the wily veteran, Surrey. As the armies came in sight of each other on 9 September 1513, James committed the deadly error of allowing Surrey to place his army between the Scots and their road back to Scotland. His final error was to order the Scots to leave their position upon Flodden Hill and toil over marshland to attack the English. Superior technology again was decisive, not archers this time, but guns, and the English infantry armed with 'bills'—short spears with axe heads on their shafts. With their bills the English broke the Scottish spears and were able to close in upon the tight Scottish ranks. The Scottish right, under Argyle and Lennox broke; the left, under Huntly and Home were victorious, but pursued their beaten adversaries, allowing Surrey to close in upon the king

Battle of Flodden

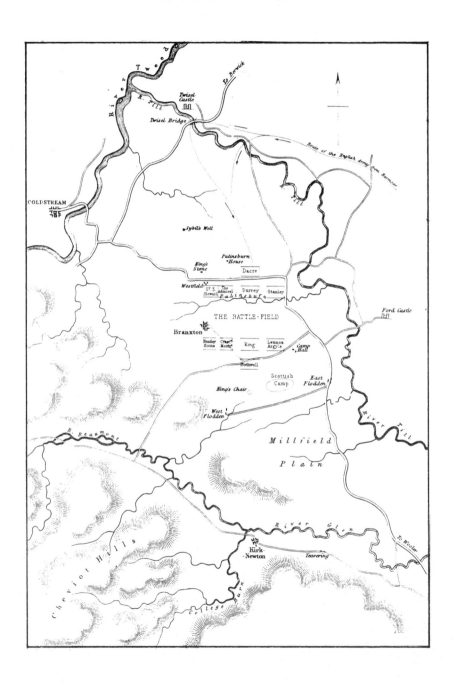

and the Scottish centre. There king James died with an English arrow in his throat and a bill wound on his head. Around him lay twelve Scottish Earls; his young son Alexander, Archbishop of St. Andrews; fifteen lesser lords and clan chiefs, and several thousand of his countrymen. They fought on till darkness fell, and then made for the Tweed and home. The road to Edinburgh lay open, and the city authorities learned of the disaster from Randolph Murray, captain of the Town Guard who had gone to Flodden and alone had survived.

Never was there such a disaster. Hardly a family in Scotland had escaped bereavement, and a whole generation of leaders had died in one afternoon. The new king, James V, was aged eighteen months.

Edinburgh's city leaders hastily built the Flodden Wall, and prepared to endure English attack, but the victory at Flodden had not been without cost, and Surrey was not in any position to press home an attack upon Scotland. So the crisis passed, and indeed an age had ended. Future English attacks would be made with some precise purpose, and no longer in any general pursuit of conquest, overlordship and the like. Things had changed in both countries, and the old medieval social patterns had begun to change with them.

In the mid 1400's there had occurred the beginnings of that remarkable process which men came to know as 'the Renaissance', when the marvellous capacities of the human mind seemed to be released and respected as never before in Western Europe. It was not perhaps really as new as it seemed. Many profound thinkers had lived and expressed themselves all through the medieval centuries, but now there was an excited feeling that man's own intellect was a marvellous gift; and that using it he

A remaining part of the Flodden Wall at The Vennel. *(Photo: Gordon Wright)*

King's College, Old Aberdeen. *(Photo: Gordon Wright)*

could examine and understand his world for himself. The natural world of science and geography was appraised in this manner; the function of literature and the arts was examined anew; philosophy as man's deepest intellectual activity was revitalised, in this new spirit of inquiry and experiment.

These ideas and events all had their impact upon Scotland. In education, two universities already existed—St. Andrews founded in 1411 under Regent Albany and Glasgow in 1451 under James II. Now, in 1495, Bishop Elphinstone founded King's College at Aberdeen; in 1496 an Act of Parliament was passed requiring landowners to have their sons trained in Latin and Law, and in 1505 the College of Surgeons was founded in Edinburgh. The Scots talent for architecture was displayed in the royal buildings of Holyrood and Falkland, Linlithgow and Stirling; and a generation—or perhaps two—of poets and authors produced a native literature in which Scots ever since can take justified pride. Robert Henryson, head of the Grammar School of Dunfermline, and, greatest of all, William Dunbar, are poets who can stand in Chaucer's company. Gavin Douglas and David Lindsay produced poetic dramas, Lindsay's *Three Estates* being of particular cultural and historical importance. The Renaissance spirit moved in Scotland, and King James had been the very model of a Renaissance prince—versatile, intelligent, cultured and progressive.

But of course, these developments were of significance mainly among the leisured classes. Study and reflection were luxuries denied to a general public, mostly illiterate, working daylight hours on the land. Their lives did not change essentially in the best part of a thousand years. Most people lived on and from the land. The entire feudal system, from highest to lowest levels, was based upon services performed in return for the use of land. The noble was bound to serve the crown as a soldier, and to bring with him tenants who were similarly bound to him. The wealth of all—crown, church and nobles—was based upon the produce of the land, worked for them by tenants. The land was worked in teams, carrying through all the processes of ploughing and sowing, reaping and threshing and milling, earning their own livelihood, and sustaining their lords by their rentals paid usually in the form of the produce of the season's work. In Scotland good, productive land was scarce, and every acre had to earn its keep every year. The 'infield' was the land which could bear a crop each year; it was ploughed and allocated, by lot and, probably, by rota, to each household contributing to the work. The 'outfield' was the land of inferior quality, which otherwise was used mainly as pasture or rough grazing. Productivity was not impressive.

The old Scots saying 'ane tae saw, ane tae gnaw, ane tae pay the laird witha' testifies to the expectation of a threefold return—one third kept as seed for the coming year, one third to feed the people, and the remaining third to go in rent to the landowner.

There were good years and bad, as always. Sometimes the produce of one harvest was consumed before the new harvest could be gathered, and people then had to scrape a living from wild plants, fish, and the like. Each year, as has been said, was a rehearsal for famine, and sometimes the famine came. Some animals at the end of each season, were preserved for breeding, and the others slaughtered, because there was not enough fodder to see all through the winter. Often the animals which had been spared were so weak that they had to be carried out to the fields when the new growth appeared on the grass. The 'lifting' became virtually an annual ritual. The slaughtered animals were salted, and the salt meat consumed as the winter dragged on. Scurvy afflicted those who made this their diet. In summer and autumn milk and cheese with meal and through time, peas and beans, gave a more balanced diet.

Class privilege affected diet and health. The landowners kept pigeons, and allowed game animals—deer and hares—to live on their land. They thus had a supply of fresh meat throughout the year and woe betide the tenant who took one of these beasts for himself.

Towns and villages developed as centres for the marketing of any surplus produce, and as bases for the various craftsmen whose skills were relevant to the land—smiths, masons, farmers, weavers for instance. Every village, every town, every city was built on some lord's land, and that lord could grant such privileges as he wished to the people of the town. This was commonly done by the granting of a charter—a document detailing the rights granted, and the obligations undertaken. These charters were proof of the bargain, and men realised fully the importance of legal proof. The men of the medieval centuries were notably concerned with legalities, and a notion of the fundamental importance of law was bred in them.

To towns granted charters to hold markets and fairs there was applied the name 'burghs'. If a burgh was on church land—like Dunfermline or St. Andrews, Paisley or Glasgow—it was an ecclesiastical burgh, its charter coming from the Abbot; if on the land of a secular lord—like Greenock or Kilmarnock—it was a 'burgh of barony'; but if its charter came from the crown, it was a Royal burgh, with special rights and status. Royal burghs held a monopoly for instance in foreign trade, import and export, which no lesser burgh could infringe; and Royal burghs sent commissioners to the Scottish parliament. Kings saw useful political opportunities, and granted charters in areas where they knew themselves to be popular. Thus King James III gave charters to many of the small towns around the Moray coast, and James IV raised improbably small Fife villages to Royal burgh status.

The Royal burghs were conscious of their superiority which they guarded carefully, and the Convention of Royal Burghs watched keenly for any challenge or any infringement.

Within the burghs there developed Gilds, whose members pursued a common trade or profession. The craft gilds—Bakers, Wrights, Fleshers—regulated standards of work, licensed apprentices and disciplined craftsmen in the public interest. At a higher social and financial level there was one merchant Gild, organising all the overseas commerce of the town.

Scots exports were very practical and showed the comparative poverty of the country. Salt and salted fish; wool and linen; hides and leather; coal—these were the products which found their way to the Netherlands, to Scandinavia and the Baltic, to France and most of all to England.

England was the only country with which Scotland could trade overland, and the biggest single Scottish export, live cattle, went to England. In days to come, trade with Europe diminished and trade with England increased, and this dependence upon English custom had profound political consequences.

Meanwhile the merchants prospered visibly. They imported fine fabrics, scents, spices, jewels and finely crafted metal, for sale to court and castle and, of course, for themselves and their families. The merchants were the sophisticates of their society, which made whatever international contacts it experienced through them.

The burghs became, therefore, more cultured, more wordly-wise, more in touch with new ideas, than the rural communities, and increasingly influential in national affairs as time passed.

A sculptured shield
including the arms of the
Guild of Shoemakers,
Canongate, Edinburgh.
(Photo: Gordon Wright)

The Queen and Mr Knox

It was to be expected that the new spirit of 'Renaissance' would quickly come to have an effect upon people's attitudes towards the church. They would ask themselves not just how they should write, or paint or trade, but also how they should think, and what the human mind could genuinely believe. From questionings came doubts; and from the doubts came theories, alternative to long-accepted beliefs, and these theories in due course brought about the disruption of the church in Western Europe. Initially there was a broad measure of agreement that the condition of the church in several respects, called for reformation. Some of those who took this view remained in the church to work for reform from within; others came to the belief that no voluntary reform could be expected, and instead broke away in the Protestant movements of Luther and Calvin. In short, perhaps the most profound effect of the Renaissance was the disruption of the church and of Christendom itself.

The Protestant movement had made considerable headway in Europe before its effects began to show with any great significance in Scotland, but once Protestant influences were carried, in print or by word of mouth, into Scotland, their spread was rapid. In any case, in Scotland, as elsewhere, criticism of the church was not really new. In 1406 the Scottish authorities had burned James Resby for heresy, and in 1433 a similar fate overtook Paul Crawar; while in the 1490's a number of people, mainly from the local gentry in Ayrshire, known as the 'Lollards of Kyle', were investigated as to their beliefs and their intentions.

During the reign of James V, a stern foe of heretics, a number of executions occurred, the most famous being that of Patrick Hamilton, burned at St. Andrews in 1528. Any martyrdom is likely to produce converts, and it was truly remarked at the time that 'the reek of Master Hamilton has infected as many as it blew upon'.

Yet heresy in doctrinal terms, however vigorously preached by committed men, was not in itself likely to turn a significant number of the general populace away from the church. Popular hostility was rather provoked by perceived defects in the organisation of the church and in the personalities and life-styles of its leading officials. The wealth of the church—ten times that of the crown itself—was a cause of discontent and envy from secular property owners; many more were antagonised not by the mere fact of wealth, but by the obsession with wealth and power and property which they believed ruled the actions and conduct of leading magnates in holy orders. The contrast between luxurious life and theoretical self-denial was particularly offensive to the many who had to contribute to make possible the enviable life-style of the higher clergy and the monasteries. David Lindsay, in *The Three Estates*, introduces the suffering and oppressed poor man, ruined by the exactions imposed upon him by the church in the collection of its traditional sources of revenue. So envy bred hostility, intensified by the widespread feeling that while the church's privileges had been well-sustained, the balancing duties and obligations had dwindled. Any privileged person or body is viewed with some measure of resentment, a measure which is increased if the privilege is seen as un-merited.

Some of the faults of the church might properly be blamed upon laymen whose cynical behaviour had helped to bring it into disrepute. Kings and nobles had used their power to place members of their families in church positions from which large incomes could be expected. Sometimes the person appointed to the position had brought competence and even—as in cases like Bishop Gavin Douglas and Archbishop Hamilton—distinction to their office; but critics noticed more immediately such appointments as those of James V's various illegitimate sons to be Abbots of St. Andrews, Holyrood, Melrose, Kelso, and Coldingham.

Even more to be condemned were appointments like that of James IV's illegitimate son Alexander, to be Archbishop of St. Andrews while he was still little more than an infant. Such appointments were seen not merely as devices to ensure comfortable positions for the lucky youths as they grew up, but as devices enabling the crown to pocket the revenues of the various religious houses while their titular heads were still minors.

Also, there had developed a practice, increasingly common from 1530 or so, for the appointment of laymen, as 'Commendators' to administer, and draw the income from, church estates and by the mid-sixteenth century, the church was increasingly seen as being defaced by corruption and nepotism in whose presence it was difficult to maintain respect. Respect for the clergy was further diminished, as the life-style of many made their vows of poverty and chastity laughable. Such personal shortcomings prompted contempt and derision among ordinary people who saw the clergy as 'idle bellies' consuming much and contributing little.

Nor were all these grievances imagination or propaganda, still less hindsight-prompted sectarian abuse. Archbishop Hamilton made strenuous efforts in the mid-1550's to reform matters; Cardinal Sermoneta, reporting to Pope Paul IV in 1556, and the Jesuit emissary de Gouda, in 1562, write of 'unbridled licence', 'avarice and neglect', and 'supine negligence'. In fact, few would now challenge the opinion, that the church in Scotland in the early and mid-sixteenth century, was in an especially unsatisfactory condition.

Yet there is one secular or political reason for hostility towards the church. The crown, in the person of James V, was committed to the suppression of heresy, but also to the maintenance of the French alliance. After Flodden, much evidence is held to indicate, the value of the French alliance to Scotland was increasingly questioned, as France seemed to gain such modest benefits as the alliance yielded, while for Scotland it seemed to bring only disaster.

To turn from the French alliance was, of course, to abandon the main principle of Scottish diplomacy since 1295; and to seem to betray so many past heroes. Scots soldiers had served with great gallantry in the armies of Joan of Arc. John, Earl of Buchan, son of the Regent Albany, had become Constable of France; the 4th Earl of Douglas, had become, for his services, Duke of Touraine, and both died for France in battle at Verneuil in 1424. So, the tradition was deeply established, and James V vigorously displayed his pro-French zeal. In 1537 he travelled, it seems uninvited, to meet personally and to marry the French princess Madeleine in Notre Dame itself; and when Madeleine died tragically within the year, it was once again to France that he turned, marrying Mary of Guise, not of the royal house but of the great family which wielded effective political power in that country.

His loyalty to the French alliance brought James to war with England in 1542, but disaffection with his policy was largely responsible for the failure of his nobles to support him with any real enthusiasm and instead to submit meekly to the shameful defeat at Solway Moss. The French alliance it could be argued, had once again brought defeat and now disgrace upon Scotland. Even James, who must already have been a sick man, did not recover from the news from the borders, and died, heart-broken they said, in Falkland. He lived long enough to hear of the birth of his one surviving legitimate child, Mary. Even this event had its depressing aspect. Mary of Guise had already had two sons, both dying in infancy, and James no doubt had hoped that the expected child would be a son. When they brought him the news of his daughter, he seems to have seen the beginning of the end of the Royal Stewarts. 'It cam wi a lass; it will gang wi a lass' he is reported to have said, with Marjorie Bruce and Robert Stewart in his mind. This daughter might rule, but any child she might have would be the child of its father, and Stewart succession in the male line would end.

The recent experience in war probably explains why the Scots did not entrust the Regency, now once more necessary, to the Queen Mother, Mary of Guise. The French alliance was rendered unpopular by defeat, and the regency was conferred instead upon James Hamilton, Earl of Arran, grandson of Mary, daughter of James II. Arran, was next in line to the infant Queen Mary, and the Hamiltons lived excitedly with this awareness for many years.

Another descendant of Mary, Countess of Arran, was her great grandson, Matthew Stewart, Earl of Lennox. Lennox had contracted a politically useful marriage with Margaret Douglas, daughter of Margaret Tudor and grand-daughter of Henry VII of England. Lennox and his masterful wife had an infant son, Henry Stewart, Lord Darnley. Mary Stewart, Arran and Darnley, together with an illegitimate son of James V, James Stewart, later Earl of Moray, were soon to become the leading personalities in the political turmoils which lay ahead.

Arran's appointment as Governor was not pleasing to the French whose favour naturally was extended to Mary of Guise. For the moment Mary, and her close ally Cardinal Archbishop Beaton of St. Andrews, allowed Arran to shoulder the responsibilities of power, in a time of considerable trouble.

In July 1543, Arran negotiated with Henry VIII the Treaty of Greenwich, whereby the infant Queen of Scots would marry Henry's heir,

Mary Stewart and the English Crown

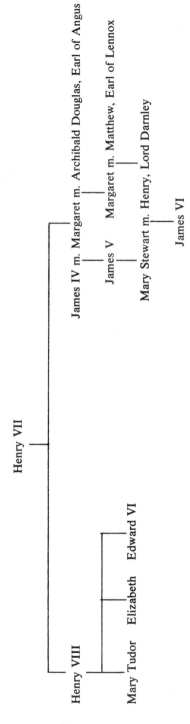

Henry VII

Henry VIII ——— Margaret m. Archibald Douglas, Earl of Angus

Mary Tudor   Elizabeth   Edward VI

James IV m. Margaret m. Matthew, Earl of Lennox

James V

Mary Stewart m. Henry, Lord Darnley

James VI

Edward. This agreement was repudiated by the Scots, and in 1544 and 1545 English armies ravaged the south of Scotland in campaigns which grim humourists called 'The Rough Wooing'. Traditional enmity to England and friendship for France naturally revived, but at this point the pro-French party lost much goodwill because of Cardinal Beaton's persevering attack upon heresy.

In March 1546, there was burned in St. Andrews, George Wishart, a Protestant preacher and missionary, who had made himself widely popular. The death of Wishart, like that of Patrick Hamilton, aroused intense anger, directed especially against Beaton, who had watched from his palace window as Wishart died. On 29 May, a gang of Protestants, mainly from Fife, fearing that Beaton might move against them and infuriated by Wishart's execution, broke into the Cardinal's palace and murdered him. They then withstood a siege of several months, during which the assassins in the castle were joined voluntarily by a small but irascible Protestant preacher from Haddington, John Knox. Knox had acted as a kind of bodyguard to Wishart and was naturally embittered by his master's death. He demonstrated his opinions deliberately by joining the 'Castilians', and was captured with them when French forces eventually compelled surrender in July 1547. His punishment was to serve as a slave oarsman on the French galleys in the Mediterranean for close on three years.

Meantime Henry VIII's death in 1547 had brought his son Edward VI to the English throne. The English Regent, or Protector, Somerset, who had been in charge of the 'Rough Wooing', now returned to the attack, and inflicted upon the Scots under Arran the crushing defeat of Pinkie, in September 1547. Arran's position was gravely weakened, and the influence of the Queen Mother rose. She decided in 1548 that her daughter should go to France for safety, and in 1554 Arran yielded the Regency to her, being comforted in his political misfortune by the French title of Duke of Chatelherault.

Scotland therefore passed under the control of a French Queen Regent. She was aided by a French Vice-Chancellor, a French Controller, a French adviser, and a French army. There is little wonder that tongues wagged to such effect that in 1555 the Scottish Parliament passed an 'Act against speaking ill of the Queen's Grace and of Frenchmen'. In 1557 the girl queen of Scots was married to Francis, the heir to the French throne, entering into secret bargains which effectively promised the virtual annexation of Scotland by France. Four members of the embassy which conducted the discussions in France died on their way back to Scotland, and there were suspicions that their deaths had occurred because they were unwilling to support the French plan for Scotland's future.

At this point the Queen Regent, who had not given any signs of being a bigot or a persecutor, allowed the execution of another Protestant martyr, the eighty-year-old Walter Milne. It seemed as though the government was now bent on an offensive against the Protestant faction and when the Queen Regent summoned leading Protestant ministers to come to confer with her in Stirling, the Protestant leaders announced their intention to defend their preachers by force of arms, and the 'Congregation' as they styled themselves, assembled in military style in Perth in 1559.

There followed a period of virtual civil war. Mary and her supporters with a French garrison, held Edinburgh and Leith, and proved too strong for the Lords of the Congregation to dislodge them. The Congregation, unable to deal with the French professionals by themselves, appealed to the new Queen of England, Elizabeth, and an English fleet arrived in the Forth, placing the French garrison in a position of no little difficulty. Negotiations for peace began, and with the death of the Queen Regent in June 1560, the French party was ready to abandon its struggle. In July, under the terms of the Treaty of Edinburgh, all foreign forces were withdrawn from Scottish territory, and the Scots were left to work out just where power in the country now lay.

Looking back on these events it is clear that three Scottish institutions—the Crown, the Catholic Church, and the French alliance—were so closely involved one with the others, that they would stand or fall together. Popular hostility to one would adversely affect the standing of the other two. A Church already under severe criticism, and a French alliance increasingly seen as being of dubious value had combined to bring the Crown into virtual civil war. It now remained for the Crown to become unpopular in its own right.

The death of Mary of Guise and the withdrawal of French forces from Scotland left the initiative in the hands of the Lords of the Congregation. In August 1560 the Scottish Parliament attempted a settlement of the religious issues. A Confession of Faith, Protestant in character, was accepted; Papal authority over the church in Scotland was renounced and the celebration of mass was forbidden. The reformers had a plan for the future structure and financing of the reformed church. The First Book of Discipline, submitted to Parliament in 1561, proposed a church, presbyterian in structure, financed by a share in the revenues of the old church. But these proposals were rejected by Parliament, and no clear plan for the new church was at this stage agreed.

This result was clearly a disappointment to the doctrinal Protestants among the reformers, particularly, perhaps, to the secretary to the Congregation, John Knox. Knox had distinguished himself during the conflicts of 1559-60 by vigorous and inflammatory preaching which had provoked at least one major disturbance, in Perth. By 1561 control of the Protestant camp lay rather with the nobles and gentry who had emerged as the leaders of the Congregation, and who were much less committed to root and branch reform than Knox. In 1561 a new complication arose.

Mary Queen of Scots, in France since 1548, and married to the Dauphin in 1558, had become queen consort in France when her husband became King Francis II in 1559. In 1560 this young woman, still only eighteen, was in a position of quite remarkable importance. She was by birth Queen of Scots, and by marriage Queen of France. Most important of all perhaps, not least in her own eyes, she was by one reading of the rules—and a very justifiable reading at that—the rightful ruler of England. A look at Mary's pedigree reveals why this was so. Henry VIII's six marriages had produced three children. The child of his first marriage, Mary Tudor had reigned from

Statue of John Knox at the High Kirk of St. Giles, Edinburgh. *(Photo: Gordon Wright)*

1553 to 1558, following her half-brother Edward VI, child of Henry's third marriage. The son had followed his father, quite in accordance with succession custom. His death while still young and childless brought to the throne Mary, his older half sister. But what should have happened after Mary's death was by no means clear. In the event the throne had gone to Elizabeth, child of Henry's second marriage, but her claim was open to serious question. Even assuming that she was Henry VIII's child—and even Henry sometimes appeared to wonder—the marriage of her parents had been able to take place only after her father's divorce of his first wife. Not only that, but though Henry had married Anne Boleyn before their daughter Elizabeth was actually born, the child had clearly been conceived in adultery, at a time when her parents were decidedly not free to marry, and she was therefore by English law illegitimate.

If this argument were to be accepted, then Henry VIII's legitimate line would have been extinct, and the throne of England would pass, rightly and properly, to the nearest family, the descendants of his sister Margaret Tudor, wife of James IV, mother of James V and thus grandmother of Mary Stewart.

In short, for any who did not recognise Henry's divorce, or who detected legal inadequacy in Elizabeth's birth, Mary was in fact the true Queen of England. And the next in line after her was Margaret Tudor's grandson by her second marriage, Henry Stewart, Lord Darnley. So it is not really helpful to speak or think of Mary as having some sort of claim to the English throne, or to be thought of as just a possible successor, some day, to Elizabeth. In the eyes of many, including probably herself, she ought

Mary, Queen of Scots, artist unknown 'detail' *(Scottish National Portrait Gallery)*

already to have been Queen of England. In this fact lies the key to Mary's tragedy.

Mary's moment of greatness did not last long. She was Queen in France for only one year, as her husband died in 1560 leaving her a nineteen-year-old widow at a court in which she had shone, but which was now controlled by her mother-in-law, the masterful Catherine de Medici, who had never liked this Guise girl anyway. So it was that in August 1561 Mary returned as queen to a Scotland changed politically almost beyond recognition since she had last seen it as a five-year-old child in 1548.

Daughter of a French mother, product of a royal French upbringing, wife and widow of a French king, Mary was French for all practical purposes. To return to Scotland—to exchange the glamour and splendours of the French court for a fog-shrouded Leith and the modest luxuries of Holyrood House, must have been for her an occasion of great depression. What is remarkable, though too often ignored, is how well she played her new role in the early days of her reign. She was good-tempered and conciliatory towards the dominant Protestant nobles, reaching with them a civil understanding that her religion was her own private affair, which did not at all threaten the move towards Protestantism which had occurred. Her chief guide was her half-brother, Moray, a shrewd and capable politician who would have been an admirable successor to his father if only James V had seen fit to marry his mother. Between them Mary and her brother maintained a tactful conciliatory policy, making for national unity; and Mary's personality, lively and charming, contributed to greater tolerance and harmony all round.

One nagging problem was always present. Mary was only entering her twenties. She would without doubt marry again sometime, even if only for political reasons. The question was, who would be the bridegroom? Many anxious eyes watched to see what would happen. France and Spain, seeing her as a Queen of England, were concerned about her choice. Elizabeth, keenly aware of Mary's menace to her position, was on the alert for any marriage which might further threaten her security. At home the Hamiltons, between whose leader and the throne stood only Mary, wondered if she might perhaps marry Chatelherault's son. Matthew Lennox and Countess Margaret thought similar thoughts on behalf of their son Darnley. Moray, reflecting on fate's injustices, knew that any husband would oust him from his sister's side; Protestant lords feared, and Catholic lords hoped for, a Catholic marriage which might begin to bring the country back to the old faith. In 1565 Mary made her choice, a disaster from which all her later troubles sprang. For what seem beyond doubt to be purely romantic reasons she married her cousin Darnley, thereby antagonising everyone important except the Lennoxes. Moray and the Hamiltons were embittered; Elizabeth saw in this marriage of her two nearest heirs all the signs of a conspiracy, while to Protestants in Scotland this Catholic marriage was a challenge.

Knox in particular denounced the marriage, loudly and publicly. He had already had several brushes with Mary, criticising her conduct on various occasions. She had tried to charm him as she had all her other critics, and had tried to make him agree that a Queen was not to be spoken to, or about, in a fashion which might suit people at a humbler level. If Knox had any criticisms, would he please meet her privately, and give her the benefit of his views? To this his response had been, 'I am not appointed to come to every man in particular to show him his offence'. In other words, public rebuke was for queens as well as for dairy maids, a point of view which Mary could probably not understand let alone accept. When Knox denounced her marriage, describing Darnley as an infidel who would go far to banish Christ Jesus from the realm (and) bring God's vengeance upon the country, Mary in a rage summoned Knox and, towering over the little man from her own six feet in height, she demanded, 'What have you to do with any marriage? or what are ye within this commonwealth?' Knox answered, 'A subject born within the same, madam'. A leading modern historian has remarked that modern democracy was born in that answer. He exaggerates slightly perhaps, but he has a very real point.

There were here brought into sharp contrast two opposing views of royal status and royal power, which were to dominate the story of Mary's descendants from that moment until they lost the throne forever. A monarchy bent on preserving and enhancing its own status and powers came into increasingly bitter conflict with those who wished to extend rights of participation. The confrontation between Knox and Mary can be seen as the beginning of the great constitutional struggle which is the story of the seventeenth century. Mary's son, James VI, carried forward his mother's views and his son Charles I and grandsons Charles II and James VII pressed them to the point of civil war and revolution.

The rest of Mary's story is briefly told, though many writers have made volumes of it. Her marriage with Darnley, offensive to so many, became within a matter of months offensive to her too. He was, to put the kindliest possible gloss upon his conduct, immature. Mary turned for friendship to her secretary David Rizzio. Protestant extremists feared Rizzio's influence, and Darnley suspected infidelity; so he and a Protestant faction murdered Rizzio in Mary's presence, and in circumstances which left Mary convinced that they had intended to cause the miscarriage of the child which she was shortly expecting. Darnley then tried to return to Mary's good graces by assisting in the attempt to punish the other murderers. Rizzio was killed in March 1566. In December his murderers were pardoned, and returned to Scotland, where they might be expected to repay Darnley for his treachery.

Early in 1567 Mary appeared to reconcile herself to Darnley, arranging for him to leave Glasgow, a Lennox stronghold, and come to Edinburgh where she could be near him during an illness which had come upon him. On 9 February she left her whining husband ill in his temporary home at Kirk o' Field House in Edinburgh, while she went to a ball at Holyrood. During the evening Kirk o' Field House blew up, and Darnley's body was found in the garden, propped neatly against a tree, strangled.

A Douglas group, followers of James Earl of Morton, were the probable culprits, but a suspect too was James Hepburn, Earl of Bothwell. In April Bothwell carried out an apparent abduction of the queen, whose friendship towards him had already caused gossip, and in May they were married.

If the Darnley marriage had cost Mary support, this latest act of unwisdom cost her her throne. The bereaved Lennox, the twice-ousted Moray and most of the nobility now rose in rebellion. She surrendered to the rebels, requiring only that Bothwell be allowed to go unmolested into exile, and became a prisoner, guarded by one of her father's former mistresses, in Loch Leven Castle. Her abdication was then extorted, in favour of her son

The Palace of Holyroodhouse, Edinburgh. *(Photo: Gordon Wright)*

James VI, with Moray to act as Regent.

To remove Bothwell was one thing. To enforce the Queen's abdication was another; and a powerful group of nobles, Protestant as well as Catholic, returned to Mary's support, achieved her escape from Loch Leven, and faced the Regent and his forces at Langside. The Hamiltons fought for her, as did Argyle and Eglinton; and even after her final defeat Edinburgh Castle was held for her by Kirkcaldy of Grange, who once already had experienced a siege when he shared in the murder of Cardinal Beaton in St. Andrews Castle. Altogether, in spite of all her errors of judgement, Mary was supported at the last by nine earls and eighteen lords, who preferred her to the alternative before them.

Mary in her flight thought obviously of France, and her first attempt was to make for Dumbarton, in Hamilton hands, from which she might escape by sea. But Moray's army barred the road north and west, and she turned instead to seek asylum in England. As a refugee, and then a prisoner, she remained for almost twenty years, while Elizabeth, with busy impertinence, took it upon herself to inquire into the Darnley murder and Mary's general conduct. Mary had been a threat to Elizabeth since her birth, and even as a prisoner, a threat she remained. Inept plots were mounted by English Catholics, prompting the English Parliament to lay down the death penalty, not only for plotters, but for the intended beneficiary of any plot. In 1586 the last—the Babington Plot—was exposed, and Mary was revealed to have been in touch with the plotters. For this she was condemned to death.

Elizabeth was unwilling to have an actual sovereign executed as a criminal. She preferred murder, and tried to persuade Mary's jailer to see to that, but he, with regard for the law greater than that of his queen, refused. So there was no alternative left to Elizabeth. Doing her best to make it all look like an unfortunate accident, she gave her consent and the Queen of Scots was beheaded in Fotheringay Castle on 8 February 1587.

Meanwhile in Scotland John Knox had preached at the coronation of the child James VI in July 1567. In 1570 he had to preach again, this time at the funeral of the Regent Moray, victim of a Hamilton assassin. In 1572 he preached his last sermon in Edinburgh on 9 November, and on 24 November he died. His last reading was from St. John, chapter seventeen, finding in Christ's farewell to his mission and his followers, an exemplar for his own. His task had been as he himself put it, to instruct the ignorant, comfort the sorrowful, confirm the weak and rebuke the proud, by tongue and lively voice. No doubt he was most himself in instructing and rebuking, rather than in comforting and confirming, because he was a positive and combative man in troubled times.

It is a pity that later sectarian prejudices, or a public opinion widely indifferent to religious zeal have led many to form a picture of Knox as a bigot, a sour sabbatarian, a destroyer of joy and an enemy of beauty. His bigotry was no greater than that of any committed partisan; he was, as his writings show, a man of considerable humour; and the sourness of later Scottish religiosity was the work and legacy of later men. Described as the one truly great man produced from the people since Wallace, he has a much better claim than most to the description.

The Crown and the Covenants

James VI has been presented in popular historical tradition as a figure of fun, uncouth in appearance, a coward and a fussy and foolish pedant. 'The wisest fool in Christendom' is one of the better known historical judgments on any political personality. This caricature is just that, and is the work of English writers who found James's alien ways amusing when he came to be among them. Judged by his record he was one of Scotland's most successful rulers. Taking full power himself, in theory, in 1580, and in practice from 1582-83, he concentrated on two main tasks—to increase national prosperity and to settle the church. In both he met with reasonable success, though his church settlement was always under threat.

In pursuit of commercial improvement he pursued a mildly protectionist policy intended to give encouragement especially to textile production— wool and linen. Export of Scottish wool was prohibited and the import of dyes and oils useful in cloth-making was freed from customs duties. Foreign craftsmen were encouraged to enter the country to pursue their own profit and to train Scots in the skills which they could display. The country's finances were more efficiently managed and the Crown's income increased by the annexation to the crown of lands which in past ages kings had given to the church. James now reclaimed them.

King James VI & I, artist unknown 'detail' *(Scottish National Portrait Gallery)*

Edzell Castle. *(Photo: James Halliday)*

Administration of justice was conducted with zeal and efficiency as always in areas like the Highlands where the years of unrest in the state had undone much of the work of James IV. Highland chiefs were required to find sureties for the good behaviour of their subordinates, and had to produce evidence for their right to hold their lands. New burghs were established at Campbeltown, Inverlochy and Stornoway. An attempt to introduce settlers from Fife into Lewis and Harris was not a success, the murder of some of the incomers by displeased islanders proving a deterrent to the recruitment of others.

Politically James's reign saw growth in the status and importance of Parliament. In 1587 the shires were granted the right to representation, and an increasing amount of business was now transacted in Parliament, where shire and burgh representatives were present, rather than in the Great Council of which they did not enjoy membership.

The result of these policies—and the diplomatic policy of peace and conciliation which went with them—gave to Scotland the first reasonably enduring period of prosperity for many a year. In this atmosphere optimism was possible, and Scottish merchants and gentry felt it safe once again to build houses which were not likely to be demolished in civil disorder or English invasion. Sir David Lindsay's castle at Edzell, and Sir George Bruce's 'Palace' at Culross belong to this period, and stand as rather touching reminders of how ready Scots were to respond to any reasonable prospect of peace and private happiness, both so long denied.

But, of course, controversy there was, particularly over the development of the church. When James came to the throne, and throughout the period of his minority the church was something of a mongrel. It was not Catholic, as Papal authority and the Mass had both been rejected; but equally it was certainly not Presbyterian. Bishops and Abbots still remained among the

'The Palace', Culross. *(Photo: James Halliday)*

clergy and many were still Catholic in their own personal opinions. In 1572 a compromise was agreed whereby bishops were to be retained and nominated by the crown, but to be examined and accepted by committees of reformed ministers; and the bishops were to be subject to General Assemblies—the Presbyterian highest church authority—in matters of belief and teaching.

In the mid 1570's this compromise was attacked by the Presbyterian faction in the church led by Andrew Melville. In 1578 Melville's Second Book of Discipline offered a Presbyterian structure to the church; and in 1580 the General Assembly, meeting in Dundee (consistently since the 1550's a centre of Protestant militancy), condemned the office of bishop as unscriptural and unacceptable. The General Assembly of 1581, meeting in Glasgow, confirmed the Dundee decisions and seemed ready to move to adopt a full Presbyterian pattern. But for this to be done the state would have to approve the changes, and this the king and Council were not prepared to do.

At this point politics intruded upon religious debate when in 1582 the General Assembly was so unwise as to record its approval of the seizure of power and the king's person by the extreme Protestant faction led by the Earls of Mar and Gowrie. The success of this Raid of Ruthven (the king had been held in Ruthven Castle) was short-lived and the Presbyterian hopes were dragged down in defeat together with the faction which the Assembly had unwisely supported.

There followed for the next twenty years or so a process of ebbing and flowing as Assemblies and Parliaments moved nearer to Presbyterianism or further from it. The king, however, had made up his mind.

Intellectually he rejected the Presbyterian pattern, largely because it was at total variance with his concept of monarchy. James believed himself, like all monarchs, to be chosen by God, and saw himself therefore the proper leader of his people in their religious as in their worldly lives and practices. This idea of royal supremacy was wholly unacceptable to Presbyterians who believed, theoretically at least, in equality of all worshippers in the eyes of God. They rejected any distinction between clergy and laity, or any hierarchy in the church. James and Melville had a memorable confrontation on this very issue in 1596, during which Melville seized his king by the sleeve, for emphasis no doubt, calling him 'but God's silly vassal' and informing the outraged James that in the kirk, the kingdom of Christ, 'King James the Saxt, is nocht a king, nor a Lord, nor a heid, but a member'. James never forgot that incident which clearly convinced him that Presbyterianism and monarchy could not co-exist.

In 1597, taking clever tactical advantage of the General Assembly's request that the church should be represented in Parliament, James agreed promptly, and invited the bishops to serve in Parliament as the church's representatives.

This was the position, when in 1603 Elizabeth of England died and James, who had painstakingly cultivated good, humble relations with the English queen, was called to the throne to which his mother had aspired. She and Darnley had been Elizabeth's rightful heirs, and now their son enjoyed the inheritance.

Enjoyed is the right word to use. There was no such thing as a 'Union of the Crowns'. The king of Scots merely, and personally, inherited an additional office, which paid much better than his old one. The two kingdoms were in no sense united, and Scotland was left in the hands of managers while her king went off to better himself. In England his standard of living was higher. The respect accorded him was vastly superior to anything he had experienced in Scotland. In England, monarchy James found, was more like what monarchy should be. And furthermore, he could now put Presbyterians in their place.

One of his first acts as king of England, was to summon to Hampton Court delegates who would devise for the church in England a structure to which all would be asked to conform. At the conference one delegate was unwise enough to mention some merits for Presbyterianism. 'A Scottish presbytery', said James ('somewhat stirred' as the report tells us), 'as well agreeth with a monarchy as God with the Devil .... Jack and Tom and Will and Dick shall meet and at their pleasures censure *me!* .... I will apply it thus, my lords the bishops .... if once you were out and they in place I know what would become of my supremacy. No bishop, no king'. And with that statement of principle and political conviction, King James presented the challenge which cost his grandson and his family the throne. For the rest of the century, if any man was hostile to episcopacy he must be ready to extend his hostility to the crown, and to expect hostility in return. Similarly, if anyone were to seek to limit royal power, he must be prepared to face the hostility of the episcopal establishment. Just as James's mother and grandparents had entangled the crown with the Catholic church and the French alliance, so now James and his successors had bound monarchy and

Clan and Family Lands

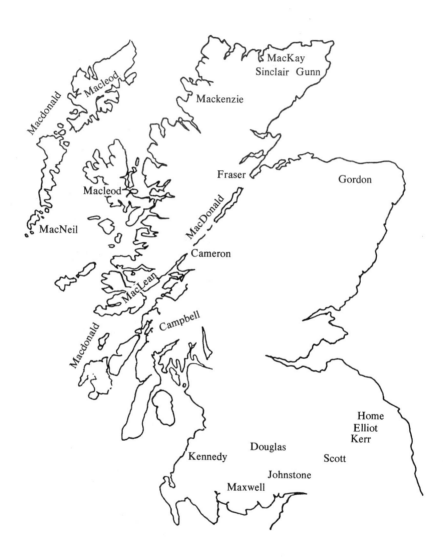

episcopacy into a political alliance which none could see to break.

While events went his way in England, James was able to take pride in the state of affairs in Scotland. 'This I must say for Scotland, and may truly vaunt it; here I sit, and govern with my pen, I write, and it is done; and by a clerk of the council I govern Scotland now which others could not do by the sword'. James's very absence from Scotland was really an advantage. Free from pressures and arguments he simply passed on his wishes to his officials, who saw them carried out. But James had qualities of shrewdness and administrative cunning which had given his Privy Council in Scotland tasks which were manageable and goals which were attainable. When he died in 1625, and was succeeded by solemn and politically incompetent Charles I, it quickly became clear that the success of James's system could be attributed in the end to the man who devised it.

Charles shared his father's notion of Divine Right, and his belief that kings should be immune from the kind of criticism and correction appropriate for lesser mortals, but he had none of his father's understanding of how far and how fast he could go in pursuing his objectives. He wanted to enhance the wealth and status of the church as it now existed, with its episcopal structure. He wanted to bring order and conformity into that church, and he chose to help him Archbishop Laud of Canterbury, one of these tidy-minded souls who see some virtue in having everyone do the same thing in the same way at the same time. Uniformity was the aim of Archbishop and king, and that uniformity they wished to extend to Scotland as well.

Charles's financial requirements had aroused annoyance among landowners, and his deference and favour shown to churchmen, including his appointment of Archbishop Spottiswoode to the office of Chancellor, annoyed the nobility who had grown accustomed to seeing politics treated as a secular activity in which laymen might expect any preferments. In 1634 the Scottish Parliament presented to Charles a 'Supplication' in which grievances were stated, and the king was invited to alter his political course. Obstinate and self-righteous Charles would not budge. In 1637 heated controversy arose over the use of the new Prayer book which Charles now required to be used in Scottish churches. The response of the Scots in February 1638, was to produce the National Covenant. It is a long, and in general, dull document, but its signatories bound themselves to maintain the form of church government most in accord with God's will (Presbytery in other words) by force if necessary. This is what made the Covenant a revolutionary document.

From the challenge there sprang the Bishops Wars of 1639-40, and in seeking to provide himself with the strength necessary to put down the Scottish rising, Charles had to call into existence his English Parliament which alone could provide him with the money which his planned military campaign would cost. He found that the House of Commons would grant him money only upon conditions, and this began the series of events which culminated in the outbreak of Civil War in England in 1642.

The conflict in Scotland soon merged into this Civil War, as Scottish factions found themselves taking sides and making alliances with their

The National Covenant of 1638. *(Edinburgh City Museums)*

English counterparts. In 1643 the majority faction in Scotland, supporters of the National Covenant, entered into an agreement with Charles's English adversaries whereby a Scottish army would be sent to assist the Parliamentary forces receiving in return a guarantee that, if the king were defeated, Presbyterianism would be not only secured in Scotland, but imposed in England and Ireland as well. To this agreement was given the name of 'Solemn League and Covenant', and in pursuit of this improbable objective a Scottish force played a major role in the defeat of the Royal army at Marston Moor, which effectively lost Charles the North of England.

Other Scots too, however, were active in the king's cause. When the Bishops' Wars began there was a very united front against the king; but a civil war which aimed at the defeat of the king and a threat to the monarchy as such, roused conflicting opinions. James Graham, Marquis of Montrose, was Presbyterian in sympathy, and had been a leading signatory of the National Covenant. He had shown himself a vigorous and gifted military commander during the fighting in Scotland, but he had come to realise that his colleagues were aiming not just at a Presbyterian establishment, but at a drastic curbing of the power of the king, if not indeed the actual destruction of the monarchy. His suspicious hostility was aroused in particular by the behaviour of the nobleman who had emerged as leader of the Covenanter party, Archibald Campbell, Marquis of Argyle. With very little encouragement from the king, Montrose formed a Royalist army in Scotland and, with assistance from Alistair MacDonald—'Colkitto'—and his men from Ireland, he inflicted upon the Covenant's armies and upon Clan Campbell, a series of crushing defeats. Despite his successes—at Tippermuir, Kilsyth and Inverlochy—Montrose's brilliance was not enough to win against the battle-hardened Scottish forces which, withdrawn from England, met and destroyed the Royalist army at Philiphaugh. Royal defeat at Naseby virtually ended the war in England, and Charles surrendered to the Scots in their camp at Newark. His hope, possibly, was to play off the Scots against their Parliamentary allies, but he was unsuccessful. The Scots, albeit with reluctance, and under what amounted to threats, surrendered their prisoner and left England. They were unwise enough to accept their expenses for their costs in the war, and provided jibing Royalists in years to come with the jingle 'Traitor Scot, sold his king for a groat'.

While in custody, Charles maintained contacts with many of those moderate opponents who did not feel happy to see Scotland under Argyle, and England under the religious extremists, who were increasingly influential in Parliament. One such group of Scots, under the Marquis of Hamilton, invaded England on the King's behalf but were crushed by the English army at Preston in 1648. It was this episode which cost Charles his life. He had invited on to English soil a foreign army, and many hundreds of Englishmen were now dead who would have been alive but for his actions. Pointing to what in another person would have been treason, the English military leaders were able to have Charles put on trial and executed in January 1649.

The execution of the king proved to be a mistake of the first magnitude. The Scots, feeling perhaps responsible for Charles's fate, and aggrieved because they had not been at all consulted, now changed sides. The King's heir was recognised as Charles II on condition that he would observe the National Covenant and the Solemn League and Covenant. This action brought upon the Scots an English invasion led by England's foremost military leader, Oliver Cromwell, who crushed the Scots at Dunbar. In one last desperate fling, the young Charles II, crowned the King of Scots by Argyle himself, conducted a counter invasion of England only to see his army broken at Worcester. Charles fled into exile, and Cromwell and his generals proceeded to conquer Scotland. A victory at Inverkeithing, and the successful storming of Dundee by General George Monck, gave England military control, and for the first time ever English forces really had conquered Scotland. Scotland was incorporated into the English state and Parliamentary system, there to remain, until the death of Cromwell, and political confusion in England prompted General Monck to lead his army to London, and call the survivors of the English Parliament into session to resolve the crisis. That Parliament, as Monck knew it would, invited Charles II to resume the throne, and the monarchy was thus restored in 1660.

The now victorious royalists, in both England and Scotland, came back to power with natural thoughts of revenge. All those who had played any part in the revolutionary successes were seen as beaten traitors upon whom retribution might properly fall. In Scotland, the major target was Argyle. He had certainly changed sides and supported Charles II, but this was not sufficient to erase royalist memories of the other actions, including the defeat and execution of Montrose who had made a more genuinely royalist attempt to claim Scotland for Charles II in 1650. Argyle now followed his great rival to the scaffold in Edinburgh.

Revenge was now carried out by legislation. The Restoration meant more than simply the return of the monarchy. By the Rescissory Act in 1661 all legislation passed since 1633 was declared null and void. This meant that both the Covenants were renounced, and an Episcopal church was re-established. Episcopacy had three crucial features—hierarchy of Bishops; lay patronage (the right of landowners to appoint the parish clergy) and royal supremacy (the king as 'head' of the church). By 1669 specific Acts of Parliament had restored all three features.

What was now to become of those who refused to accept the new arrangements? Parish ministers were ordered to submit themselves for reappointment by the new Bishops. Some 300 refused, and were 'outed' from their charges, their places going to men prepared to serve, enthusiastically or resignedly, within an episcopal system.

Crown policies and episcopal church government were now more clearly than ever closely inter-connected, and opposition to one inevitably involved opposition to the other. A convinced Presbyterian now found it difficult to be an obedient subject, and a man's religious zeal could almost be measured by the extent of his disloyalty to the king.

Those whose consciences prompted them to disobedience began by refusing to attend church services held under the new authority, attending instead services conducted by an 'outed' minister. This disobedience was met by a series of fines. Non-attendance at the official services was punished by a fine; attendance at non-official services was punished by another fine. These non-official services were conducted in private houses or premises, and became known as 'conventicles'. Everyone attending a conventicle was liable to a fine; and heads of families were held responsible for the behaviour of their dependants. In due course they were even held responsible for the behaviour of their tenants or servants. The fines were on a scale so harsh that a family incurring them all would very rapidly be economically ruined.

So, secrecy became desirable, and conventicles came to be held not in private buildings, but in the open air, in some spot remote enough to avoid detection. Outed ministers were compelled by law to move twenty miles from the pulpits which they had previously occupied, and, as conventicles continued, a new law provided that ministers conducting such services were to face the death penalty. Thus there now began another great national—or at least local—tradition; ministers fugitives, with a price on their heads, worshippers in breach of the law, and armed guards protecting the conventicles against the possibility of attack from royal military patrols. When death is the penalty to be faced, then hunted men and their defenders

The Covenanters' Prison, Greyfriars Kirkyard, Edinburgh. *(Photo: Gordon Wright)*

will more readily inflict death upon their pursuers.

The actual holding of conventicles was not in itself the major cause of worry to the authorities; officials' anxiety was aroused rather by what was there said and discussed. Sermons tended to deal with contemporary issues, albeit thinly disguised as commentaries on events recorded in the scriptures. 'Preaching to the times' was how they put it. Villainous rulers in ancient Israel, and biblical examples of tyranny and persecution, were used to teach lessons which were not lost upon the congregation. So discontent simmered, conventicles continued, and patrolling soldiers policed the disaffected areas, notably Fife and the south-western countries. John Graham of Claverhouse, one of the military commanders, once remarked irritably that there were in Galloway 'as many elephants and crocodiles as there are loyal and regular persons.'

If discontent and sedition smoulder away for a long period the instinct of governments is usually to try to bring the unrest out into the open where it can be crushed. By 1677 the authorities were frustrated and infuriated by the prolonged nature of Presbyterian resistance to which there seemed no foreseeable end. From the Bishops there came the suggestion that the restless areas should suffer some 'notable corporal punishment *in terrorem*' which would probably provoke a rising, expose the ringleaders, and 'render them inexcusable'. With this aim there was dispatched into Ayrshire in the spring of 1678, an army of irregular soldiers recruited from the estates of Royalist lairds and nobles of Angus and South Perthshire, to which history has attached the rather misleading name of 'The Highland Host'. They were to maintain themselves by confiscation—living off the land in military terms—an army of occupation in effect. The result for the south-west in loss

The Traditional Territories

The Covenanters' Memorial, Rullion Green. *(Photo: Gordon Wright)*

of produce, financial damages and physical assault and intimidation, was considerable.

But, there was no rising. The whole object of the exercise had failed and by the end of the year the Highland Host was withdrawn. At this point when the attempt to provoke rebellion had failed, events played into the hands of the government. On 3 May 1679 a group of extremist Presbyterians in Fife ambushed and murdered Archbishop James Sharp of St. Andrews—a vigorous supporter of royal policy, a zealous extorter of fines, and, as former parish minister in Crail, a turncoat enjoying enormous unpopularity. The murder had disastrous consequences. The murderers fled, some of them to seek shelter with friends in the west, and the royal dragoons went looking for them.

Thus it was that, on 1 June, Claverhouse and a small force came upon a large conventicle at Drumclog on the Lanarkshire/Ayrshire border. Believing that some of the assassins were in the congregation, Claverhouse attacked, but the conventiclers proved strong enough to beat him off. Rebellion was now a fact. Government forces mustered in Glasgow, and Presbyterian recruits came forward to join the rebel army which now openly stood for 'The Good Old Cause' of the Covenants. An army, generally accepted as being from 4-5000 strong, faced the Royalist force under James, Duke of Monmouth, one of the King's sons, across the Clyde at Bothwell Bridge on 22 June. The result was disastrous for the Covenanters. Disunited and squabbling, they failed to prevent the advance of the royal army and their ranks were speedly shattered.

Bothwell Bridge gave the government all the advantages that had for so long proved elusive. Presbyterians could now be treated as virtual traitors, and moderates and extremists alike had to submit to the triumphant severity of the Crown and its instruments. The main body of Presbyterians was cowed and submissive, and 'The Good Old Cause' was dead as far as the mass of the population was concerned. Resistance continued, but it now came only from a tiny minority of extremists—and potential martyrs.

Victory and Surrender

Resistance to the crown in the years following the Battle of Bothwell Bridge was offered only by the most extreme Presbyterians, and those extremists tended also to be the least influential in social and economic terms. Both circumstances encouraged the king's agents to adopt the harsh measures, which have earned for these years the name 'The Killing Times'. Who were killed, and why? The leaders of the resistance were frank in their oratory and prolific in their writings, and there should be no difficulty in understanding what happened. On 4 June 1680, there was circulating a manifesto of resistance, the 'Queensferry Paper', wherein it was claimed that 'We shall no more commit the government of ourselves, and the making of laws for us, to any one single person or lineal successor .... aptest to degenerate into tyranny as sad and long experience has taught us .... If we shall be pursued or troubled any further in our worshipping, rights and liberties .... we shall look on it as a declaring war .... and seek to cause to perish all that shall in hostile manner assault us'.

The Queensferry Declaration was followed within a matter of days by the Sanquhar Declaration of 22 June. The Sanquhar document announced that its sponsors 'disown Charles Stuart. We do declare a war with such a tyrant and usurper .... and against all such as have .... sided with or in any wise acknowledged him in his tyranny'. In other words, the men who issued these statements were talking politics, and the politics of treason.

The Queensferry paper was the work of Donald Cargill, former minister of the Barony Church in Glasgow, banished to live North of the Tay in 1662. For close on twenty years he was one of the leading field preachers until his capture near Lanark in July 1681 and his execution shortly thereafter. The Sanquhar Declaration was read at the town cross by Richard Cameron. In 1680 Cameron was thirty-two, a native of Falkland, educated at St. Andrews and in October 1679, he became a leading organiser of, and preacher at, conventicles. He was thus a hunted man even before his demonstration at Sanquhar, and the king's soldiers were hot on his heels. On 22 July Cameron, with sixty-three followers, was caught and attacked at Airds Moss, near Sorn. As the troopers charged upon them Cameron prayed, 'Lord spare the green and take the ripe'—and died there at the head of his little army.

Cameron's name came to be applied to those who still continued to defy and resist. Presbyterians were in general cowed and silent. Even 'Covenanters' is too wide a term to apply to the resisters. Instead, they came to be identified as 'Cameronians'.

Leadership of the Cameronians was taken up by James Renwick whose 'Apologetical Declaration' of October 1684 defined the king and all his servants as 'enemies to God and the covenanted work of reformation', to be punished as such. Following upon this latest pronouncement, soldiers were empowered to administer to any suspect, an oath whereby the suspect disclaimed all support for this Declaration. Any who refused the oath were shot on the spot. Thus the Killing Times happened. The martyrs shot or drowned by the army, or arrested and hanged, suffered not for their religious beliefs, but for the political rebellion into which their religious beliefs had led them.

The chief official in Scotland as the Killing Times proceeded was the king's brother and heir, James, Duke of York and Albany. James, a convert to Catholicism had fallen victim to an anti-Catholic political crisis in England in 1679, and had been sent to Scotland as Royal Commissioner to get him out of the way as that crisis was dealt with. He thus became identified in Scotland as having responsibility for the worst persecution of the Cameronians. This reputation was quickly recalled when in 1685 Charles II died, and James succeeded to the thrones of the two kingdoms.

His accession was greeted by another Sanquhar Declaration, which described the proclamation of James as 'choosing a murderer to be governor, who hath shed the blood of the saints of God'. The Cameronians were not alone in their misgivings. Moderates were in the next few years, turned into extremists by James's policies.

In 1688 English politicians, deeply hostile to his conduct of government, were prompted to immediate action by the birth to James's second wife of a son who would succeed his father, and continue a dynasty of Catholic kings. A conspiracy involving powerful English politicians, of varying political beliefs, was formed to bring James under their control. To assist them in this enterprise, they invited the ruler of Holland, William of Orange, to come to England with an armed force sufficient to reduce James to obedience. William's readiness to accept the invitation was confirmed by the fact that his wife, Mary, was James's elder daughter, who would have succeeded her father but for the birth of this unexpected and inopportune son. He had long anticipated the day when his wife would succeed in England; and English money, English ships, and English influence would be available for his use in his life's work, which was to save Holland from France.

So he responded to the invitation, landed in England, and prompted James to escape into exile in France. After some confusion the English Parliament conferred upon William and Mary the joint sovereignty of their country. What now would the Scots do?

Just as in 1660 royalist triumph in England had delivered Scotland into royalist hands, so now events in England offered the Scots a chance to escape from those particular hands.

The Convention of Estates which met in Edinburgh on 14 March 1689 had three options. They could stand by the exiled James; they could follow the English lead and give the Scottish crown to William and Mary, or they could accept neither, and instead try to create a republic. There is substantial evidence to show that many of them would have liked to have a republic, as many men had come to believe that all kings were liable to become oppressors, but the practical difficulties were too great for most to regard the republican option as realistic. But they could agree upon the next

Location of Events

best thing, which was to make the future monarchy as like a republic as possible.

They agreed that they would follow England's lead, and offer the throne to William and Mary, but upon conditions. *If* the new sovereigns would take a Coronation Oath, whose main point was to pledge to maintain a Presbyterian form of church government; *if* they would accept the Claim of Right, rejecting James's religion and the various repressive actions of Charles II and James; and *if* they would promise redress to a list of grievances, including the Episcopal essentials of prelacy, patronage and royal supremacy over the church, *then* they would be accepted. The first two conditions were quickly accepted, and William and Mary became king and Queen of Scots.

Two struggles, one military and one political, now followed. Those who had wished to stand by James, and had seen their wishes over-ruled, now turned to attempt a military counter-revolution. The leader was John Graham of Claverhouse, upon whom James had conferred the title of Viscount Dundee. Leaving the Convention, in which he had been out-voted, and leaving Edinburgh where his life was in danger from the many friends, relatives and supporters of his late victims, Dundee turned north to raise an army for King James. Thus came into being the political faction which sought to restore King James and his dynasty, to which attaches the name Jacobites (from the Latin *Jacobus*, James).

By July, Dundee was active in the Atholl area, and the new government in Edinburgh sent a force north to deal with him. Just north of Killiecrankie Dundee shattered the army of General Hugh MacKay, and opened the way south to Perth and thence to Edinburgh. But Dundee himself was dead,

Scene of the Battle of Killiecrankie, 1689. *(Photo: James Halliday)*

killed in the battle. The Jacobite command passed to Colonel Cannon, a professional soldier and a good one, but lacking the brilliance of Dundee. Still, the politicians in Edinburgh expected the Jacobites to be among them at any moment, and many panic-stricken departures took place. MacKay's army was broken and no force seemed available to stand in the path of Cannon and his men.

But one force did exist; a force of volunteers, highly motivated and with a fierce, cold hatred of King James and all he had stood for. A regiment had been raised from the ranks of the persecuted Cameronians; and that regiment, under its Colonel, William Clelland, took up position in Dunkeld and stood there to receive the Jacobite attack when it came. So, the two extremes of Scottish politics confronted each other. They fought for everything in Dunkeld—for hedges, ditches, walls, houses, roofs and rooms. It was a savage battle because it was an ideological one, a classically bitter and vicious civil war in miniature. Clelland died, but his men held Dunkeld, and the Jacobite force retired, dispersed and ceased to exist. The Cameronians survived, to become a regiment in the British army, with their depot and recruiting zone in the Lanarkshire and Ayrshire moorland towns and villages, in which their traditions had begun.

The political struggle took longer. The Coronation Oath and the Claim of Right had been quickly accepted by William, but he was not at all ready to redress the Grievances. The second 'Grievance' was royal supremacy over the church, and this William would have preferred to retain. The first, significantly, was the Committee of the Articles, by means of which kings had controlled parliamentary business. The simple truth was that William did not wish to give up any royal powers, having as much sense of his own importance as any of his predecessors. He and his supporters argued that however bad past kings had been, William was good and trustworthy, and would not abuse his powers. The view of the majority in the Convention was that any king left with the power to oppress was always likely to become an oppressor, and the present chance to diminish royal power must be taken. Only after a year of political manoeuvring was William forced to admit defeat, and in May 1690 the hated committee passed out of existence.

The result was that the Scottish Parliament was free of royal dictation, passed on from London to obedient officials for implementation. It was free to develop policies and to decide on issues. It was free to take initiatives in diplomacy and commerce. All of its plans could be made with what were judged to be the best interests of Scotland in mind.

One might have thought that such a happy state of affairs would endure virtually for ever. But what if the best interests of Scotland were not the best interests of England? And if the Scots pursued their own best interests regardless, how would England react?

The immediate concern facing the officials of the new government was to ensure, as far as they could, good order throughout the country. Dundee's rising had given them a severe fright. First Montrose, and then Dundee had been able to use the Highlands as a source of recruits for armies with which possibly to coerce the government and politicians in Edinburgh. It was natural that peace in the Highlands was a prime objective of William's administrators. The question was how best that objective might be secured. The first method which they tried was bribery. The Earl of Breadalbane, chief of the Campbells of Glenorchy and northern Perthshire, was given money—£6000 we are given to understand—with which to bribe chiefs into a happy relationship with the new regime. Breadalbane unfortunately, was a quite outstandingly devious and unscrupulous person, and he gave priority to bribing himself. And why not? The result was that when he and others met to discuss the distribution of incentives the meeting broke up in accusations and recrimination.

Having used the carrot, and found it inadequate, the government now decided to use the stick. All Highland chiefs were to be required to take an oath of loyalty to William before New Year 1692. Any who refused would find themselves victims of traditional 'fire and sword' punitive expeditions. It was thought probable that the pride or honour of some of the chiefs would make them openly defiant. The king's Secretary of State in Edinburgh, John Dalrymple of Stair, (once Lord Advocate to King James before a timely change of sides) had high hopes of catching in the net one or other of the most defiant of the MacDonald chiefs, Keppoch or Glengarry.

As the months passed and oaths were duly taken, the sheriffs sent their reports back to Edinburgh, where, in early January, Dalrymple and his colleagues excitedly began their scrutiny of the documents. To their dismay they found that no chief had refused. Deeply incredulous and frustrated they re-examined, and found a flaw in the submission of MacIan MacDonald of Glencoe, who had gone to Fort William to take the oath only to find that he had to go instead to Inveraray. As a result his oath was taken after the deadline set. He was not quite Keppoch or Glengarry, but he would do, and so instructions to the appropriate army officials were sent, ordering them to proceed against MacIan and his clan 'to burn their houses, seize or destroy their goods or cattle, plenishing or clothes, and to cut off the men'. 'Men' were defined on these occasions as males between the ages of seven and seventy. 'It will be a proper vindication of the public justice to extirpate that sect of thieves' was Dalrymple's opinion.

The story of Glencoe is sadly familiar. Parties of soldiers guarded each end of the glen, while another was sent in to live in billets among the MacDonalds until the time came to carry out their orders. Their story was that they were merely pausing in the glen for a little while before moving on towards the Keppoch and Glengarry areas. On 12 February, Major Duncanson gave the official orders to the Captain of the forces in the glen, Robert Campbell of Glenlyon. If only Glenlyon had had another surname much misunderstanding would have been avoided in later years. Because he was called 'Campbell' virtually everyone who knows about Glencoe assumes it to have been just another clan battle. The fact that such a notion is nonsense has proved insufficient to alter public perception, and those really responsible have enjoyed a quite unearned alibi.

Glenlyon did as he was told. MacIan, his wife, and most of his clansfolk were shot and stabbed during the early hours of the morning. His son led a party of survivors over the mountains and the snowdrifts to find refuge among the Stewarts of Appin to the south and west of Glencoe.

Glencoe, scene of the massacre in 1692. *(Photo: Tom Weir)*

News travelled slowly, and not until late in the year were rumours heard in Edinburgh of the massacre; and not until the meeting of Parliament in 1696 was there any opportunity for proper investigation. There was then nothing much to be done, as King William had personally signed the orders placed before him by Dalrymple. The latter was for the moment removed from office, but he returned before very long. And that, except for memory, was the end of the matter. Lowland politicians, though they would use what material they could to embarrass opponents, were not really greatly concerned about the fact of the MacDonalds, and in any case blame could be successfully shuffled off on to the Campbells. But no one really had any doubt as to where blame really lay. The MacDonalds were slaughtered, not by a rival clan but by regular soldiers, servants of the state, in the king's uniform, on the instructions of the king's Secretary supported by the signature of the king himself.

Glencoe, then, never provoked the political crisis which it might properly have done, and for the remainder of the 1690's the Scottish Parliament was preoccupied with more material concerns.

Ever since 1603 the Scots had cherished the hope that they might be allowed, as subjects of the same king, to share in trade with England's colonies, but the English, like all colonial powers of the time, would never dream of granting any such rights. Colonies were seen as assets to be monopolised for the benefit of the country to which they belonged and all interlopers were fiercely excluded.

James VI had tried to organise some sort of fuller union of his two kingdoms, but the English were not in the least interested. On numerous occasions Scottish Parliaments hopefully appointed committees to negotiate union with England, but the English were not interested.

Anxious to diversify and expand their trade, the Scots now embarked upon an alternative approach. If they could not gain access to England's colonies why should they not simply establish colonies of their own? Such colonies would be a source of raw materials, a market for Scottish produce and a base for her ocean-going traders. Thus the Scottish Parliament encouraged and authorised the formation of 'The Company of Scotland Trading to Africa and the Indies', and the Company would establish a colony as its base and the beginnings of a Scottish commercial network. Such a venture would require large sums of money. A fleet would have to be organised, equipped, provisioned and provided with cargoes. Scotland did not really have the amount of capital to make such investment, but help was at hand. England's laws excluded, from England's colonies and markets in large areas of the world, even English merchants who were not members of the great East India Company. The influence of that company was vigorously maintained by many members of the House of Lords and several hundred members of the House of Commons. Englishmen who were not in the East India Company had chafed for years over their disadvantage. But the English Parliament had no jurisdiction whatsoever over a Scottish company, and so many English merchants gleefully and legally rushed to invest in the Scottish company. Dutch merchants followed suit and the Company of Scotland looked like being a great success.

At this point the 'East Indiamen' in the English Parliament awoke to their danger, and belaboured William with demands that he stop the Company of Scotland; or if that was, for some reason which escaped them, impossible, then he must forbid English subjects—or Dutch subjects—to invest in the Scottish venture. Under severe parliamentary pressure William agreed, and by English law Englishmen were now forced to withdraw from the enterprise.

The Scots at this point would have been wise if they had stopped to reconsider their plan, but pride was now involved and in an astonishing outburst of patriotic defiance they now subscribed enough money to make good the sums withdrawn by English and Dutch defectors. At what a cost to the country became in due course apparent.

Comparatively poor and humble people bought one share, or would join with others to make a collective purchase of one share.

By an amazing national effort the necessary funds were raised and the preparation of the fleet carried out. The Directors of the Company had selected the site of their colony. It was to be on the Isthmus of Panama, at a spot called Darien, where North and South America met and where the Atlantic and Pacific met. Darien was as near to the world's crossroads as one could imagine. It seemed strange that no one was there already. What they did not appreciate was that the climate of the area, and the hazards to health from fever and all possible tropical infections, had deterred the Spanish, who were in control of the surrounding area, from actually occupying Darien. However, if any outside power showed interest, Spain would certainly oppose them.

Monarchs of a United Scotland

Duncan I	1034-1040	Robert II	1371-1390
Macbeth	1040-1057	Robert III	1390-1406
Malcolm III	1057-1093	James I	1406-1437
Donald Ban	1093-1097	James II	1437-1460
Edgar	1097-1107	James III	1460-1488
Alexander I	1107-1124	James IV	1488-1513
David I	1124-1153	James V	1513-1542
Malcolm IV	1153-1165	Mary	1542-1567
William (the Lion)	1165-1214	James VI	1567-1625
Alexander II	1214-1249	Charles I	1625-1649
Alexander III	1249-1286	Charles II	1660-1685
Margaret of Norway	1286-1290	James VII	1685-1688
John (Balliol)	1292-1296	William (of Orange)	1689-1702
Robert I (Bruce)	1306-1329	Anne	1702-1714
David II	1329-1371		

The Stone of Scone.

In July 1698, seven ships sailed from Leith for Darien. Their cargoes included heavy textiles—canvas, linen, serge, homespun cloth and blankets. They carried also shoes, stockings and slippers; wigs, Bibles and Kilmarnock bonnets; oatmeal and twenty-nine barrels of clay pipes. Clearly they had much to learn about trading in the tropics, trading with native Indians, and the unwisdom of carrying Protestant Bibles into a Spanish-influenced area.

The first fleet landed; established a base called Fort St. Andrew, and proclaimed the new colony of New Caledonia. Soon fever struck; the natives proved unfriendly, and a Spanish expedition prepared to march against them. They hung on doggedly, twice being ready to evacuate but each time inspired to stay because reinforcements reached them in two fleets, one of two ships from Leith in May 1699, and a third of four ships from Rothesay in September 1699. But the Spaniards closed in upon Fort St. Andrew. The Scots sent pleas for help to the English governors—subjects of King William like themselves—of Jamaica and Nova Scotia, but the governors were under orders to give no help whatever. William needed the goodwill of the English Parliament, and he wanted also to maintain friendly relations with Spain. The Scots therefore were left to surrender to the Spanish force whose commander, impressed by the brave conduct of Campbell of Fonab and the Scottish garrison, allowed the starved, half-dead survivors to march out in honour, leaving their country's colonial ambitions in ruins.

Because hopes had run so high Scottish bitterness over the Darien disaster was correspondingly great. Financial ruin had come upon thousands, and in their distress and their anger Scots singled out English ill-will as the major cause of their tragedy, and feeling against England and King William ran high.

At this point, with friendship between the two parliaments and peoples at a particularly low ebb, the English Parliament in 1701 moved to deal with a problem which had been causing them much concern. The marriage of William and Mary had been childless, and Mary was now dead. Mary's sister Anne, younger daughter of King James, was next in line according to the law of England, but her children all had died in infancy, except for the Duke of Gloucester who survived for a few years. So there was a succession problem, and the English Parliament in 1701 passed the Act of Settlement to provide for an orderly succession when the need arose. All Catholic claimants—the son and descendants of King James for instance—were debarred. William was to reign until his death, after him Anne, and after Anne, if none of her children survived, was to come Sophia of Hanover, daughter of Elizabeth Queen of Bohemia and grand-daughter of James VI.

The Scots observed the English action and saw an opportunity to apply pressure. They had no more desire than had their English counterparts to see the restoration of the Stewarts, but the English Act had been passed without any consultation with the Scots, and once again English politicians had revealed an arrogant assumption that whatever England did, Scotland would automatically accept. In their bitterness over Darien and their irritation at this latest high-handed action by the English, the Scots turned

Later Stuarts and the Hanoverian Succession

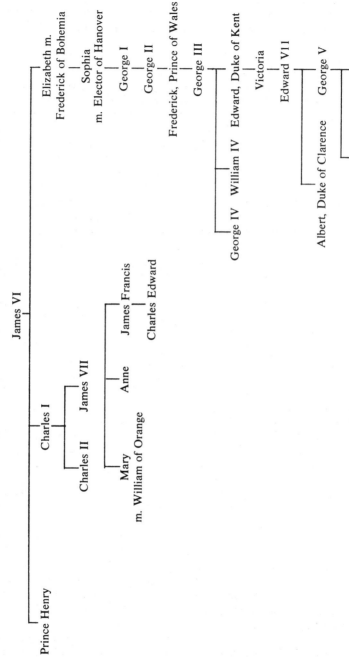

their minds to the possibility of blackmail. The Protestant succession and the guarantee that the Stewarts were gone forever were the two fundamental needs of English politicians. If the Scots were to play upon these fears they might perhaps extort commercial concessions which England had for so long denied them. Thus, in 1703, the Scottish Parliament passed the Act of Security which stated that on the death of Queen Anne, Scotland would not accept the same monarch as England unless Scots were granted equality of access to England's colonial markets. If the Scots persevered, and carried their Act into effect, England faced a choice between two unattractive alternatives; either the Scots would breach her monopoly of her colonial trade, or a Stewart king, with French friends, might be back in Edinburgh. Strategically the two countries might be back in 1560, with Scotland a base for French mischief-making to England's detriment.

It was not very likely that such an event would really come to pass, Scottish memories of the Stewarts from 1660 onwards being as they were. They probably gave the identity of their possible separate monarch no serious thought, in the belief that things would never be allowed to reach such a stage. They were quite right, though hardly in the way they expected.

They had forgotten that blackmail is a game that two can play, and that England might find some way to counter Scottish plans. The English answer was brutally effective.

By the terms of the English Alien Act of 1705 the English moved 'for the effectual securing the kingdom of England from the apparent dangers that may arise from several acts lately passed by the parliament of Scotland'. They had two telling blows to deal the Scots. Firstly, all inheritance of property in England by Scots would cease; and secondly, all English purchases of Scottish goods and produce would cease, as from 25 December 1705, unless by then, the Scots had agreed to the terms of the English Act of Settlement and the Hanoverian succession. The first condition was a severe jolt to the Scottish nobility and gentry who held property in England; the second spelt economic ruin for Scotland. The dangerous consequences of over-dependence upon England as a market for Scottish goods, and the neglect and decay of trade with other European countries, were now starkly apparent.

The Scots had no alternative now but to come to some sort of agreement. The English offer went part of the way to meet the Scots' ambitions. Yes, the Scots could trade in future with England's colonies, but in order to earn this benefit they would have to surrender their independent parliament. One parliament would now serve both kingdoms, and the Scots would merely have representation in the parliament in London. On this basis, the Scots agreed to begin discussions in London, while for their part, the English government concentrated an army under General Wade at Newcastle, indicating that conquest was a possible outcome if the Scots should too long delay in coming to terms.

To describe the discussions as 'negotiations' is to misuse language. Each day began with the English delegation placing before the Scots the proposal to which their consent was that day required, and the English thereafter went about their ordinary business leaving the Scots to wrangle among themselves. When the proposals emerged the English Parliament passed them without opposition and with no great interest. For the Scots the debate was in the fullest sense historic. They were deciding whether or not they could, or should, attempt to maintain their political identity or, in other words, their independence. One side concentrated on the fact that Scotland's nationhood was at stake, while the other essentially argued that Scots had no alternative under such economic pressures; and that in any case, a defiant, independent Scotland could not in the future prosper. No one mentioned General Wade, but everyone knew where he was, and why he was there.

When the Scots came to vote on 16 January 1707, the vital first clause was carried by 116 to 83. The final vote, to accept or reject the Act of Union as a whole, was carried by 110 to 69. The majority is clear, though when looked at more closely opinion was not quite so one-sided. The nobles voted 46-21 in favour of the first clause, and 42-19 on the final bargain. Corresponding figures for the shire commissioners were 37-33 and 38-30; and for the burghs 33-29 and 30-20. The more popular representatives, in other words, were fairly evenly divided, and the convincing majority was provided by the lords.

Many Scots, at the time and since, have attributed the behaviour, of the nobles at least, to bribery; and others have piously deplored any such suggestion. The truth is that in the eighteenth century any parliamentary decision

Parliament House, Edinburgh. *(Grant's Old and New Edinburgh)*

100

of any significance was attended by the offer and receipt of favours and inducements. That is how business, in the absence of a party system, was done. It would be an occasion for the most profound surprise to find that bribery had played no part in the making of the Union.

Argyle for instance, let it be known that he would not even attend if he was not rewarded. He wanted to be a general in the army, and he wanted a peerage for his little brother Archie. Argyle became a Major General and Duke of Greenwich. Lord Archie became Earl of Islay, and a much better politician than his brother.

Atholl was promised arrears of expenses due to him if he made no trouble. Tweeddale would receive his arrears if his behaviour was satisfactory. The Treasurer-Depute was entrusted with £20,000 for distribution to the deserving. Like Breadalbane in 1690 he rewarded himself with £1200 and distributed the rest with reasonable skill, earning government thanks for 'my service in the Union Parliament'.

In the new—if it was new—Parliament, there would sit sixteen Scottish peers and forty-five members of the House of Commons. Coinage, weights and measures, and commercial measures generally were to be uniform throughout the completely unitary state of 'Great Britain'. But Scots Law was to continue as before, and the Presbyterian structure of the Church was guaranteed. Thus was secured the goodwill of two powerful vested interests which might otherwise have become exceedingly awkward.

The Earl of Seafield—as secretive and shifty a politician as even that age produced—presided as Chancellor over the Scots Parliament in its final moments. As he pronounced the acceptance of the Union, and the adjournment without limit of time of the Parliament, he remarked jovially 'There's an end to an auld sang'.

So Scotland was gone, and the rest of the world knew her not. For England nothing had changed. English rulers had never seriously or sincerely accepted Scotland's separate identity anyway, and the presence of Scots in the English parliament seemed to them just as it should be. Some of the terms of the Union were set aside before long when English opinion saw fit to require change. Taxes on malt and salt were imposed earlier than had been promised; and the power of landowners to appoint local ministers, abolished in 1690, was restored in 1712, to remain in the church as an affront to Presbyterian theory.

For Scotland the Union was the great historical decision in the country's story. For England nothing much had really happened and nothing important had changed. For this reason the concept of 'Britain' has never been fully accepted. As has been observed in modern times, 'If the English had become British, so might the Scots'.

Changing Scotland

Different groups of Scots adjusted to the changed status of their country in accordance with their own best interests. In Glasgow for instance, the opening to Scots traders of English colonies gave the merchants of the city the opportunity to amass great wealth from the tobacco trade between Britain and the plantations in the West Indies and the American eastern seaboard, Virginia especially. The 'Tobacco Lords' came to dominate the economy and the civic life of the city, their profits providing funds for investment in sugar and in cotton-processing and manufacture in due course. The new trading links with the New World were soon to alter completely the centuries-old trading pattern of pre-Union times, shifting the country's main commercial activity from the east coast to the west. From the early post-Union years until very recently, commercial and industrial Scotland centred on Glasgow and the Clyde.

The effect upon Edinburgh was different, but equally striking. The loss of political purpose in the capital might have been expected to create something of a ghost town, but in fact Edinburgh flourished as never before. Its University in particular, like its sister institution in Glasgow, became a centre of excellence in a whole range of studies—arts and sciences alike. Scottish philosophers, like David Hume and Adam Ferguson, were recognised throughout Europe and America as the foremost original scholars of their time.

Edinburgh came to be called 'The Athens of the North', and the city enjoyed an intellectual and cultural 'Golden Age'. Physically the city was transformed, thanks largely to the vision and energy of George Drummond, a leading figure in local politics and Lord Provost for several terms. Buildings designed by architects of international status gave grace and dignity especially to the New Town, built across the newly drained Nor' Loch; and the New Town became Scotland's finest example of the expression in stone of the spirit of the age.

That spirit is summed up in terms like 'The Age of Reason' or 'The Enlightenment'; terms which remind us that the eighteenth century saw a flowering of human imagination and talent unsurpassed since Renaissance times. Just as then, in the fifteenth century, so again in the eighteenth, men drew inspiration from classical examples. In architecture, in philosophy, in literature and the arts, even in gardening, emphasis was upon symmetry and order. The inspiration was scientific. Scientists observed that the world operated in accordance with rules which Mathematics and Physics could test and prove. The notion that the world was essentially founded on harmony and order encouraged the desire to show form and order in all human artefacts, and encouraged also the optimistic belief that life and society could similarly be planned and ordered if only men would use their

Edinburgh's New Town from Edinburgh Castle. *(Photo: Gordon Wright)*

intelligence. There developed an optimism; a confidence that Man by the exercise of his intellect, could improve himself and his institutions, and perfection itself was not an impossible goal. It was all a far cry from the conflicts and emotionalism of the seventeenth century, but the obsessions and issues of that period had ceased to be relevant. The preoccupation with church government had lost its urgency with the settlement of 1690; while the old magic, mystical monarchy by Divine Right had gone with the Stewarts, and King William and King George were magistrates and administrators, rather than embodiments of God's will.

The new age would, however, have been unlikely to come to birth but for one further consequence of the Union. The aristocracy—the 'natural leaders' of the Scottish political community, had not abandoned their political ambitions or their taste for public life. There was now a new state to be served and a new, richer paymaster, from whom rewards for service might be expected. Those who would be courtiers had to go to the Court, and the Court was now in London. So to London went the Scottish aristocracy.

With that regard to the interests of their descendants, which is an acquired characteristic of aristocracy, the Scottish nobles now saw to it that their sons would in future be educated, according to English usage, in England, from whose schools and universities the English state had drawn its servants, just as the new British state would assuredly do. By residence, by up-bringing, by social contacts, by participation in public affairs, the Scottish aristocracy became thoroughly integrated, within a generation indistinguishable from their English colleagues. They deserted, more or less

103

en masse, the people they had led and the culture which with them they had shared.

Into the social gap thus left, there came the new men of significance, their claims to power and influence resting upon their talents and their intellect and not upon their pedigree or their acres. The new men were lawyers, university professors, leaders of professions and men distinguished by success in commerce. These men were preoccupied by the wish to construct and to improve. Diplomacy and statecraft now belonged to London, and Scotland's new men were concerned with the intellectual and commercial activities which remained in the Scottish community.

The vigour and influence of Scottish cultural life was spectacular, and not merely in the abstract. Practical consequences flowed from the theories and ideas which abounded. However, before these practical developments could fully come to pass, Scotland had to pass through one last crisis, one last expression of the old seventeenth century controversies.

It was to be expected that some attempt would be made to set aside the Act of Settlement in order to secure the restoration of the branch of the royal family which had been excluded by Parliamentary decision, but which was, by blood, the rightful line. Such attempts were now made by the supporters of the old traditional monarchy to bring to the throne James Francis Edward, son of the ousted King James (who had died in exile in 1701). For thirty years Jacobite hopes endured, bringing about more or less constant diplomatic negotiations and political intrigues, and, in particular, two armed risings aiming at the restoration of the Stewarts.

The attempts concentrated especially upon Scotland. Support for the Jacobite cause in England was negligible, but in Scotland emotions were more extreme and more contradictory. In most of the Lowlands the Stewarts were hated and feared, though some families among the nobility and gentry, mainly because of Episcopalian or Catholic commitment to Divine Right, were sympathetic. In the Highlands support was proportionately rather greater. The Campbells were Presbyterian and Hanoverian, and this had the effect of making clans who were their neighbours and victims—usually the same thing—take the opposite side. So Macleans, Stewarts of Appin, Camerons and MacDonalds of various septs, were receptive to Jacobite appeals, to which in any case the religious views of the chiefs of these various clans inclined them.

Further north, away from Campbell pressures, there was less interest. Mackays, Sinclairs and Gunns were as Hanoverian as the Campbells, and the Mackenzies were not especially interested one way or the other.

So the balance of opinion in the Highlands was fairly even, with perhaps, if we exclude Clan Campbell, a slight tendency towards Jacobitism. In the country as a whole there was no doubt that the exiled line was opposed by a substantial majority. The point was, however, that, given the military potential of the clans, Scotland might just possibly be won for the Stewarts on the battlefield.

Thus Scotland became the focus of Jacobite attention; and Scottish national grievances and hurt were played upon by Jacobite supporters. 'Scotland and no Union' became a Jacobite slogan which men were in due course to inscribe upon their swords.

Some Jacobite response was to be anticipated after the accession of George I in 1714. To strike before the new regime in London had been properly settled in, and while irritation against the Union continued in Scotland, was an obvious tactic, and as soon as plans could be devised, a rising duly occurred, beginning with the raising of the standard of King James VIII, by John, Earl of Mar on 6 September 1715. The rising was ineptly led. Border Jacobites—Lord Kenmure in Galloway, and the Earl of Derwentwater in Cumberland—marched rather inconclusively in the North of England, until surrendering at Preston. Mar failed to make any well-timed or really persevering attempt to break through to Edinburgh, allowing himself to be blocked by an army a third the size of his own, led by Argyle, at Sheriffmuir on 13 November. By February 1716, Mar and James himself, who had landed too late to contribute anything much to his cause, were both in exile.

Jacobite prospects had been adversely affected in 1715 because French policy at that moment was not supportive. That policy, however, changed; by 1743 France was at war with Britain, and her rulers readier to pursue their traditional policy of encouraging disaffection which would divert British attention and power from the continental war. Thus James's son, Charles Edward, received a more encouraging response when he proposed to lead a further rising on his father's behalf. The French were never able to bring themselves to give all-out support to such enterprises, but on this occasion they did provide Charles with money, supplies and some seven hundred soldiers with which he set sail in a two-vessel fleet from Nantes in July 1745. One vessel was driven back to France after an encounter with a British warship, and it was with only seven men and no material French support that Charles landed in Eriskay on 23 July. His obvious weakness deterred chiefs who had been making Jacobite noises, but appeals to loyalty and honour from Charles won over Cameron of Lochiel, and his example brought others round. On 19 August Charles raised his father's standard again at Glenfinnan; and in due course the clans of the west-central Highlands—Cameron, Stewart, MacLean, MacDonald and various branches of Clan Chattan—together with the Episcopalian and traditionally loyalist aristocracy and gentry of the North-East, Angus and Perthshire, joined the Prince.

In September Charles took Perth and a fortnight later, Edinburgh. General Cope, who had allowed himself to be panicked out of trying to hold Charles's advance north of Perth, had brought his army by sea from Aberdeen to Dunbar, and now marched to the relief of Edinburgh. On 21 September an early morning attack by Charles at Prestonpans shattered Cope's army and left Charles triumphantly to return to Edinburgh where for some weeks he held court in Holyrood while the city became again the capital of a country over which England's rulers held no authority.

The Jacobite triumph was short-lived. Moving into England Charles attracted virtually no support. For a time the best strategy seemed to be for the Jacobites to press on towards London, where an unseemly panic developed among the great but unwarlike financial and political

Battle of Culloden

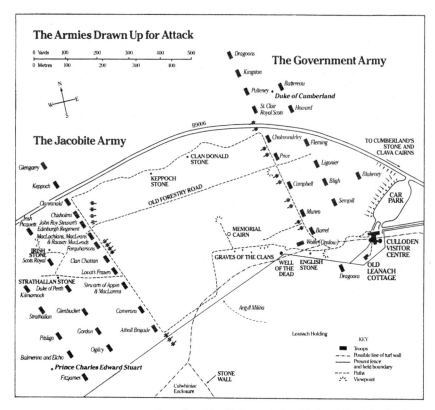

Reproduced by kind permission: National Trust for Scotland.

Looking out over the battlefield at Culloden. *(Photo: Gordon Wright)*

personalities. But facing a growing government force to the south, and menaced to his left and right by other armies, Charles had to give way to the advice of his officers—especially the one truly competent general among them, Lord George Murray—and retreat from Derby back to Scotland began on 'Black Friday', 6 December.

A revolutionary army on the retreat must always fall prey to anxiety and loss of morale, and so it was with Charles's force, weakened by desertions. It was still a formidable instrument, capable of inflicting a sharp defeat upon General Hawley, who pursued it too closely, at Falkirk on 19 January. It had some moral successes too. When the army camped overnight near Stair Castle, home of the Dalrymples, there were those who thought of taking a modest revenge upon the property, but a guard was mounted by the MacDonalds of Glencoe who thus saved from destruction the house of the man responsible for the massacre of 1692. Then again, as the Jacobites passed through Glasgow it seemed very likely that that Presbyterian and Hanoverian city might suffer for its politics, but Lochiel exerted such discipline over his soldiers that no violence was offered to the citizens or their homes.

Retreating ever northwards, pursued by the government army under the Duke of Cumberland, the Jacobite army was eventually forced to fight a pitched battle at Culloden, where on 16 April the exhausted and half-starved men in its ranks fell victim to the artillery of Cumberland, the survivors perishing in one last desperate sword-wielding charge on the enemy lines. Charles spent an adventurous year as a fugitive, protected by the loyalty and devotion of many Highlanders, until able to secure rescue in a French ship and thus escape to face the rest of his life as an exile.

For the Highlanders who had followed him, the suffering did not end with the deaths under the guns at Culloden, or at the hands of the punishment squads of Cumberland the Butcher. The whole Highland way of life was

107

now to perish, as Parliament in London devised laws which would ensure that the events of 1745-46 could never happen again. A Disarming Act legally stripped the clans of their weapons, and bagpipes and Highland dress were banned for good measure. The clansmen, who had provided the chiefs with a military capacity were no longer soldiers in waiting, or at least not on behalf of their chiefs. The Tenures Abolition Act destroyed the bond of military service between chief and clansman, and the Heritable Jurisdictions Act took from the chiefs their virtually sovereign powers over their tenants. The Highlands would now be subject to the same laws and procedures as all other parts of the British state.

During those years while the Jacobites had been hoping, planning and fighting, life in the non-Gaelic parts of post-Union Scotland had been proceeding largely unaffected by these excitements; because, with the obvious exception of the great expansion of American trade, the development of the Scottish economy had not been vitally affected by the Union at all.

When the century began, Scotland, like most of Europe, displayed all the characteristics of what would today be called an under-developed country. Nine out of ten people lived by working on the land, using methods virtually unaltered since the Middle Ages. Land was cultivated at subsistence level; its produce to be eaten rather than marketed. Such profits as the system produced went to those who owned the largest estates; and these men used their wealth, generally speaking, in self-indulgence. Brandy on their tables; silver on their garments; a coach on their terraces or another turret on their dwellings, all too commonly were preferred to financial foresight or worthwhile investment.

But the Enlightenment had a practical side to it, and the successful lawyers, academics and merchants who had emerged as the new rising class had, in many cases, marked their success in the traditional fashion—they bought land. Sometimes they found that the gentry were not willing to part with their land, but usually the market provided enough to cater for the ambitions of the new rich; and sometimes, even if purchase was impossible, marriage into aristocratic families would provide entry into the landowning world.

For these men, and for some of the traditional gentry, the scientific improvement of their estates was a favoured expression of intellectual vigour. If it was true that man could, by his own wits and energy, make his world a much more rational and comfortable place, where better could an intelligent man set out to prove his point than on his own land?

There was an economic incentive too. As the eighteenth century proceeded, a rising birth rate was creating a demand for food which agriculture, using traditional methods, could not meet. Thus intellectual promptings and commercial expectations combined to encourage efforts to increase the productivity of the land. In 1723 there was established the Society of Improvers in the Knowledge of Agriculture. The Society's members sought to encourage and sponsor experiment, and to circulate advice and reports of good agriculture practice. Their Secretary, himself a laird, Robert Maxwell of Arkland in Galloway, was outstandingly energetic in seeking to inspire and inform his three hundred or so colleagues. The Society produced a series of publications urging change, and advising as to how and where changes could be made.

The organisation of the land—the old infield/outfield system, and its communal 'runrig' working, should be replaced by enclosure, and long leases granted to encourage effort. Walls or hedges and tree plantations would provide shelter from the elements as well as protection against straying animals. The soil could be drained, cleared of peat and moss, fed with lime; thus treated, more acres could be brought into cultivation, and those already in production could be enriched.

At this early stage these activities tended to be the hobby of enthusiasts rather than the general practice of the country, and indeed the Society itself ceased to function from around 1750, by which time some Improvers had over-reached themselves. Some ideas, drawn from England and Europe had not been really feasible on Scottish soil and in the Scottish climate. Cockburn of Ormiston, who, like his neighbour, Clerk of Penicuik, was a typical Improver, bankrupted himself in his enthusiasm, and had to sell his estate.

So, progress was not smooth, but it did endure, and the enthusiasm and interest of the Improvers was to prompt and inspire landowners into enlightened estate management throughout the rest of the century. Landowners and tenant farmers alike joined in draining and weeding, treating and protecting their fields, sponsoring and purchasing new items of equipment which inventors were offering. The mechanisation of farming processes had made progress in England, and Scots farmers were increasingly using improved ploughs, seed drills, harrows and reaping and threshing machines. James Small's plough, perfected by about 1765, made extended cultivation possible, and reaping and threshing machines, devised by Patrick Bell and Andrew Meikle, made harvesting much more efficient.

Over these improvements, throughout the eighteenth century and into the nineteenth, there presided practical theorists like Lord Kames, typical of lawyer-landowners; Lords Gardenstone and Monboddo; Barclay of Urie and Grant of Monymusk—all of them, and many others, practising new techniques, and encouraging innovation. New rotation patterns were introduced, helping to ensure that land could remain more or less constantly in production, and the longer leases offered by landowners encouraged tenants to match the enthusiasm of their landlords.

The yield of the land—the ultimate indicator of success—was improved substantially; and, in stock-farming, selective breeding increased the average weight of animals four-fold, and their value five-fold.

Closely associated with agriculture were the crafts and industries which used the produce of the land as their raw materials—wool and linen for instance. These industries had been supported, from the early part of the century, by bounties and premiums paid out by the Board of Trustees for Fisheries and Manufactures, founded in 1727 (rather belatedly, as a body of the sort had been promised in Article 15 of the Treaty of Union). Throughout the century the Board acted to provide incentives for production in bounties and prizes; training for intending craftsmen and women; experts to train Scots in specialised continental methods, and encouragement to mechanisation. As in agriculture, so in these textile industries, success was proved by the vastly increased output. In the chief linen-producing areas, Fife and Angus, for instance, linen output rose from under one million yards in 1728 to over thirteen million by 1788. The processes involved in linen production were made more speedy and more efficient by rapid mechanisation. The flax plants, used in linen-making, had to be 'retted' in ponds or pits, where the soft parts of the plant would rot away, leaving the tough stems and fibres. These then were 'scutched'—pounded or beaten—to soften the woody stems, and finally 'heckled' or combed, to thin out the fibres and make them ready for spinning. All these processes were traditionally carried out by hand, but water-powered machines were devised and installed in 'lint' (i.e. flax) mills which numbered some two hundred and fifty by the 1770's. Spinning and weaving were revolutionised by the engineering ingenuity of Hargreaves, Arkwright and Crompton in spinning, and Kay in weaving. The old handcraft wheels and looms were superseded by machines powered, first, by water, and eventually by steam. In 1790 the Board of Trustees received a petition from James Ivory of Kinettles near Dundee, asking for the Board's patronage and support for his purchase of 'one of the patent machines for spinning linen yarn to go by water'. In 1794 Alex Aberdein and Co. in Arbroath had followed Ivory's example. Within thirty years there were seventeen spinning mills in Dundee alone and another thirty-two in nearby Angus villages.

Around the linen industry, pioneering in mechanisation, there also developed ancillary industries and services. Dyeing and bleaching developed in Perth; and the British Linen Company, formed to organise credit facilities for the industry, became in due course a bank, rather than a producing company.

The pattern set in the linen industry was repeated in the later development of the cotton industry which developed especially in the Glasgow and Clydeside area, from just before 1780. Cotton was the most adaptable of cloths. It could be combined with linen if that would seem likely to produce the kind of material required. It could be produced in a variety of qualities, heavy and useful for domestic furnishings, or in quality which compared with the finest linen. It was more easily processed than linen, and in due course, by the mid-nineteenth century, came to be *the* main textile produced in Scotland.

Mechanisation of industry had very far-reaching social consequences. The new machines were expensive, and beyond the pocket of most of the spinners and weavers who had kept cloth-making going as a home-based 'cottage' industry. Also, the machines were bulky, and really required special premises. For these reasons the industries passed into the hands of specialist owners, who could buy the machines and build sheds in which to instal them, thereafter paying workers to come and operate them. These 'manufactories' had to be built near the source of power—running water to begin with, and then near coal-fields when steam-power came to be used. The workers had to follow the work, and the owners of the machines and 'factories' (the shortened version of the original word) began to provide housing near the workplace for the convenience of the workers. So it came about that the old independent handloom weavers, and domestic spinners, working to commissions or contracts in their own homes, were superseded by two very different groups—the owners of machines and premises who controlled production, and the paid employees who carried it out. Thus emerged the new classes of decision-making owners, living off the profits of their industries, and wage-earning workers, operating to instructions and under supervision. Obviously the interests of these groups would clash, especially as workers sought to maximise wages and owners sought to maximise profits.

The owners were, in many cases—perhaps most—men of humble social origins themselves, with no tradition of aristocratic sense of obligation to their dependants. They were frequently insensitive, sometimes cruel, and their view of their workers created a social problem which came to loom large in the political arguments throughout the rest of the nineteenth century and beyond.

One exception to the general rule was the cotton producing complex at New Lanark, founded by David Dale and Robert Owen, well-known for his unusual enthusiasm for social experiments. Owen and Dale believed that workers who were well-treated, and who worked in healthy and comparatively pleasant conditions, would produce at least as profitably as those who were under constant threat and compulsions, working in conditions devised in such a way as to cost the owners next to nothing. New Lanark had a school, and leisure facilities for its workers, and became a work place of international fame for its attempt to humanise the new industrial relationships.

New Lanark. *(Photo: Gordon Wright)*

111

The Iron Works at Bonawe, near Taynuilt, Argyll. *(Photo: Gordon Wright)*

Fundamental to all these developments were the industries of coal-mining and iron-founding; coal to fire the boilers which produced the steam which drove the engines; coal to heat the furnaces in which iron was smelted; and iron to provide the frames, rollers, cylinders and pistons from which the new machinery was made.

An iron industry had long existed in Scotland, using imported iron ore smelted in furnaces heated by charcoal, which was in turn produced from Scottish forests. For this reason the earlier ironworks were in, to modern eyes, rather surprising places—at Invergarry, on Lochfyneside, and, most famous of all perhaps, at Bonawe, where the birch forests by Loch Etive fuelled the fine iron works.

The industry in the lowland areas took its beginnings from the creation of the great works at Carron, near Falkirk in 1759. There charcoal was fairly quickly replaced by coke, and Carron became the great centre for the production of ironware from simple domestic goods to heavy guns. The wars of the eighteenth and nineteenth centuries provided the demand for iron which kept Bonawe and Carron busy. Opportunities for profit encouraged others to enter the industry, and ironworks at Muirkirk and Wilsontown followed. When, in 1828, J. B. Neilson devised a new type of furnace which could use Scottish iron-ore, the industry saw further expansion in the Lanarkshire and Glasgow area.

Glasgow became the centre of this 'heavy' side of industrial development for many reasons. The capital which the Tobacco Lords and their successors accumulated, provided money for investment, and success bred success. Glasgow had a pool of talent and expertise in its blacksmiths and wrights, its carpenters and its clockmakers, all men whose craft skills could be, and were, adapted and used in the new setting of factories and the new style of mass production. Its University provided experimental and theoretical support, and one of its staff, the laboratory technician James Watt, was beyond doubt the most vital contributor of all to the new age of production, having made it possible for steam engines to operate with the degree of efficiency which made all the rest possible.

So eighteenth century Scotland was profoundly changed from the Scotland of the past. It was no longer a nation of rural workers and landowners, but increasingly a nation of town-dwellers and capitalist employers. It was now a nation whose future lay with Carron, not with Culloden; a nation whose appropriate emblem was not the White Rose of the Jacobites, but the blue flower of the flax.

Prince Charles Edward Stuart by H D Hamilton, 1775, 'detail'.
(Scottish National Portrait Gallery)

The Highland Tragedy

The pattern of society in the Highlands had come to differ profoundly from that prevailing in the Lowlands, but these differences have been dwelt upon in modern times rather more lovingly than the historical facts warrant. There was no particular distinction between Highland and Lowland as such in the early days of Scotland's existence. Differences were not fundamental; they developed, in consequence of certain facts of a practical nature, not from any mutual hostility, acts of will or racial distinction. The real point was that the medieval Scottish state and its rulers moved as far towards centralising authority as they reasonably could, but their success was limited by technology. Kings anxious to impose order and obedience could succeed within limited distances from the centre of royal power. At greater distances the task became increasingly difficult. Policing and supervision were more difficult to organise the further one went towards the periphery of Scotland. That is why the exercise of local independence as, for instance, by the Lords of the Isles, was feasible; and why the best that kings of Scots from Alexander II to James VI could do was to mount expeditions from time to time, to reassert the principle that the Highland areas were part of a greater whole. Between such periodic demonstrations however, the facts of time and distance took over, and power in the Highlands reverted to those who were strong enough to claim and exercise it in their own localities.

Even this feature was not unique to the Highlands. Lowland nobles often enjoyed considerable freedom of action in their own areas; and in England too, the further north and west from London one might travel, the more immunity from royal control one would find. What did perhaps make a rather different case of the Highlands was that, unlike Lowland aristocrats in Scotland, or territorial magnates in England, the Highland chiefs are found very seldom playing any significant role in affairs of state or national politics. Of the truly Highland, Gaelic chiefs, only the Campbells of Argyle were consistently involved in such matters. Partly, therefore, indifference to Council, Parliament and state business in general on the part of the chiefs was responsible for the detachment of the Highlands from the rest of the country. Detachment, arising from the facts of geography and the purposes of the chiefs, was reinforced by developments over generations. In particular, English, the language of administration and commerce, came in time to dominate the Lowlands and the eastern seaboard, but Gaelic prevailed elsewhere, and a linguistic border is a very difficult barrier to surmount.

Then, Protestantism gained the upper hand in the country, and, especially after 1690 and the Presbyterian victory, Gaelic became suspect as 'the Irish language'—a description habitually employed by the eighteenth century—and the Irish language was, by many, seen as some sort of adjunct to the Irish religion. The Catholicism of some of the chiefs had become another factor encouraging a sense of division.

In their comparatively isolated territories, the chiefs and their followers had evolved a society whose assumptions and purposes differed greatly from the rest of the country. The chief's power, and his own sense of his power, was measured by the number of followers at his command, not so much because they could be organised to raise produce for his consumption, and deploy skills for his comfort, but because they could be commanded as fighting men. The clan was essentially organised for war, not for commerce.

That is why the legislation after Culloden proved destructive to Highland society. The chiefs now had to maintain themselves as any other landowners had to do, and their lands had to be made to pay. As one observer has put it as a southern socialite the chief needed money, but as a tribal patriarch he could do little to raise it. So the clan as a kind of extended family, encouraged to think of itself communally, would have to give way to a society in which the owner of the land lived off rents, and the tenants' job was to pay these rents.

Oddly enough, in the half century after Culloden the new relationship worked reasonably well. Estates of Jacobite chiefs were forfeited to the Crown, and placed in the control of Commissioners, who carried out in the Highlands many of the improvements which elsewhere had been sponsored by the Board of Trustees, and some of the men responsible for improved agriculture in the Lowlands served terms of office as Commissioners for the Forfeited Estates.

Money was spent organising surveys and prospecting for coal and minerals; on land reclamation and afforestation; on premiums and bounties for linen and hemp production, and on public works programmes aimed at providing roads, bridges and harbours. Attempts were also made to develop a fishing industry, with villages being constructed, or reconstructed, at, for instance, Lochinver, Ullapool, Plockton and Tobermory.

So, though the chiefs had found their status profoundly changed, the economy of the Highlands did not at all collapse after Culloden. In fact there were indications that things promised to go rather well.

In 1755 more than half of the population of Scotland lived north of the Tay, and almost one third of the total were natives and residents of the Highland, Gaelic area. For the next fifty years or more the population continued to rise, in some places at a quite staggering rate. Overall, the Highland population by 1830, had risen by about 50 per cent, and in the Outer Isles it had actually more than doubled. A population growth of this sort is usually taken to be an indicator of rising prosperity and such indeed was the case.

Britain was involved more or less continuously in wars between 1742 and 1815. These wars were fought by British armies and warships in America and in India as well as on the European continent, and many Highlanders were recruited into the army, forming Highland regiments, and beginning the tradition of military service to the British crown which has endured ever since. Recruiting soldiers from among their tenants brought advantages to

The village of Plockton, Wester Ross. *(Photo: Gordon Wright)*

the landowners. Sometimes they were actually rewarded for their recruiting zeal, and, at least, if men went off to fight there were fewer mouths requiring to be fed from the produce of the estate.

Feeding the rapidly rising population on a traditional diet of oatmeal, cheese and meat was an increasing problem, as output of these items could not keep pace with the growth in numbers. One solution had been found in the humble but remarkable potato. In 1743 the Improvers had urged their members to increase production of this plant, which could produce a far greater volume of food per acre than any other crop. One of the early converts to the idea of potato-growing was the chief of Clanranald, who returned from a visit to Ireland in 1743, enthusiastically committed to potato growing. By 1800 potatoes provided 80 per cent or so of the diet of the Highlanders.

With their own people thus provided for, the chiefs were able to make substantial profits by selling the other products of their land to meet the needs of the armed forces, a vast market for meal, cheese, meat, fish, leather, all of which the Highlands provided. Also, a new product was in great demand—seaweed or kelp—which, when dried and burned, left ash which was essential to a wide range of industries, notably glass and soap production. The chemicals necessary in these industries had been traditionally imported, especially from Spain, but that import trade had been greatly impeded by the succession of wars, and a home-produced substitute like kelp was a godsend, for which generous prices would be paid. In 1720 kelp ash was selling at £2 per ton. By 1790 the price was £10 per ton, and by 1800 it stood at £22. This was a boon to landowners. Lord Macdonald was reported to have earned £20,000 per year from the kelp

116

Kelp burning in Orkney around 1900. *(Photo: Tom Kent)*

produced from the seashores of his lands, and Clanranald made £98,000 annually. The landowners controlled the new industry totally, and naturally sought to expand it.

Such expansion depended upon the willingness of the tenants to leave their fields and go kelping along the shores. This they were not always willing to do, particularly since the landowners paid wages which were absurdly low in proportion to the profits earned. The chiefs were not willing to reduce their profits by paying more generous wages to their tenants, so some other means had to be found to force the tenants to work in whatever way would bring greater advantage to the chiefs.

The first tactic was to raise rents to levels which produce of the land could not meet. The tenants were thus forced to spend time gathering and burning kelp to meet their new obligations. Secondly, and more damagingly, landowners altered the leases of their tenants, restricting the acreages of their holdings, and thus making it more necessary for them to take up some extra occupation, like kelping or fishing. In 1799 Lord Macdonald reorganised the tenures on his estates, leasing land in individual holdings too small to maintain a family. Such plans were warmly approved by professional estate managers, notably two from the other side of the country on the estates of the Countess of Sutherland. James Loch, the Sutherland factor, urged landowners to ensure that future holdings were 'of a size to induce every man to engage actively in the prosecution of the herring fishery'. His subordinate and ally, Patrick Sellar, echoed his sentiments, advising holdings 'pinched enough to cause them to turn their attention to the fishing'.

A further method employed in Sutherland and on Skye was to remove tenants altogether from their traditional lands, and grant them holdings on inferior land, by the shore, most convenient to kelping and fishing. The landowners thus gained twice. They drew vast profits from the kelping and fishing labours of their tenants, and they drew high rents from new tenants invited into the lands vacated by their former occupants. These new tenants were usually sheep farmers—'flock-masters'—mostly Lowland Scots or Englishmen who would pay well for the grazing rights in Highland glens.

117

Whatever discontent these developments caused, most landowners neither knew or cared. Forty-six Highland landowners lived on their estates, but one hundred and forty-nine were 'absentees'. As the Earl of Seaforth put it, 'What Hebridean proprietor lives in his estate that can live elsewhere?' Discontent showed itself in various ways. Some tenants sought to emigrate, as many Highlanders had done in the 1760's and 1770's. The Highlands then had been abandoned especially by the tacksmen, the traditional right-hand men of the chiefs, their overseers and rent-collectors in peacetime, and their subordinate officers when the clan went to war. For these men, especially, the post-Culloden Highlands held little, and they had left in large numbers, leading many of their people to America and Canada, or to Lowland Scotland. Though the journey to the New World was long, it was often preferred. In Glasgow and the Lowlands, the Highlander was entering an established, English-speaking community, where he would be alien. In Canada or America he and his friends could establish their own Gaelic-speaking communities.

So, emigration was seen by some as a preferred alternative to the increasing drudgery and dependence of life at home. But by now, in the early 1800's, men were valuable to the landowner, because they could earn money for him. Thus the landowners used their political influence and parliamentary power to place obstacles in the way of those who might wish to emigrate. In 1803 Parliament passed the Passenger Vessels Act, which, under the guise of enhancing safety on board ships crossing the Atlantic, set the fare for the passage at a level so high as to be beyond the capacity of escaping Gaels to pay.

The government too did not look favourably upon emigration, which might reduce the number of potential recruits. Already enthusiasm for

A family evicted from their home in North Uist in 1891. *(Photo: A. Goodrich-Freer)*

military service had declined, as resentful Highlanders, driven to small unproductive holdings and forced to engage in unwanted tasks, took a modest revenge by ignoring the pressures of their chiefs when the recruiting officers came round.

Things changed very rapidly when the wars ended in 1815. Fighting men were no longer wanted. The price of kelp fell again to £2 per ton, and landowners quickly found that tenants were no longer an asset but were likely to become a burden. Thus in 1827 the restrictions of the Passenger Vessels Act were removed, and emigration was not only permitted but vigorously encouraged.

The one promising source of income for the landowners remained the sheep farmers; and it became the policy of the chiefs to substitute sheep for tenants as quickly as possible. The Sutherland estates had pioneered the work, evicting tenants from their holdings throughout Strathnaver and Kildonan between 1799 and 1813. Now the example of Loch and Sellar was followed in South Uist and Wester Ross in the 1820s, in Skye in 1826, and in North Uist in 1828. Volunteers were encouraged to take passage for Canada and America, and when volunteers were not forthcoming, evictions and expulsions followed.

One event which had frightened the landowners was a harvest failure in 1816, which had seen the people survive on shellfish and wild plants until the 1817 crop was safely gathered. A disaster of similar sort, but on a scale undreamed of, now struck the Highlanders.

In 1845, just as in Ireland so also in the Highlands, the potato crop was struck by blight. The damage, though widespread, was not complete, and everyone relaxed until in 1846 blight struck again, and the whole potato crop was left rotting in the fields. All the consequences of famine then quickly followed. Scurvy and typhus, diseases of malnutrition, killed hundreds. The famine-stricken population, weakened and listless, fell victim to cholera outbreaks, and only help from outside could relieve the situation.

Private charity might provide some help, and so might the state, but, in the first instance, the sufferers looked to the chiefs for protection as generations of experience had taught them to do. Some landowners responded with admirable sense of obligation. MacLeod of Dunvegan bought in food for his people, some eight thousand of them, and permanently damaged the fortunes of his family by so doing. MacLean of Ardgour provided food, and introduced new crops into the area—peas, cabbages and carrots—to replace the potatoes. Sir James Matheson on Lewis spent £329,000 on improving his lands, hoping to provide a more secure future for his people.

Others did nothing. Gordon of Cluny, owner of the Uists and Barra, was later reported as 'most negligent'. On Skye on the estates of Baillie of Dochfour, 'fertile land (was) lying waste—people starving'. In Knoydart, around Arisaig, Lord Cranstoun showed total indifference to the situation, leaving attempts at relief to a tenant, MacDonald of Glenaladale, and to the parish priest, Father MacIntosh.

One who particularly disgraced himself was Lord MacDonald, who was

119

publicly denounced by the depot officer at Portree. MacDonald had bought meal, which had been made available for relief purposes, in Liverpool, but re-sold it at a profit instead of bringing it home. The government was reluctant to act. These were years when the economics of *laissez-faire* prevailed, and politicians felt unclean if they had to interfere with the workings of the market, where supply and demand should dictate the terms of trade, and where any action by the state was seen as a distortion of natural processes. The scale of the disaster was so great however that the Assistant Secretary to the Treasury, Sir Charles Trevelyan, already in charge of relief measures in Ireland, had his powers extended to Scotland as well. Using the resources of the Admiralty, depots for food distribution were established at Portree and Tobermory, supervised by an official whose name was improbably apt—Sir Edward Pine Coffin. A Central Board of Management to co-ordinate charitable efforts was established in February 1847, and from its offices in Glasgow and Edinburgh, supplies were despatched to the affected areas. A ration was fixed of 1½ pounds of meal per day for a man; 12 ounces for a woman and 8 ounces for a child. Donations in cash and in kind came from America and Canada, and by mid 1847 the crisis had passed, and the depots were closed.

The harvest showed great promise, but gales caused widespread damage, and potato blight struck again. The Board began all over again, but showing a new approach. Its members had been criticised as being too concerned for the suffering, and not alert enough to the need to keep everyone up to scratch. So now the victims had to make some gesture towards earning their rations. They were to work an eight-hour-day for six days a week in return for their meals. Meal supplies would be reduced as a punishment for any 'idleness', because, as Trevelyan put it, 'dependence on charity is not to be made an agreeable mode of life'. At the prices of the time the meal on offer to a man, his wife and six children cost three shillings and two pence per week—sixteen pence. The lowest working wage of the time was thirty pence. There seemed very little risk that Trevelyan's fears would be realised.

In 1848 and 1849 the crops failed again, and all the devices to provide work whereby meal might be earned became more and more absurd for half-starved people. In 1850 the Board's funds were exhausted, and its members simply announced that its activities must end.

So, at the last, responsibility for the people fell again on their own social leaders, the landowners, who were now faced with having to pay extra local rates—the Poor Rate—of almost six pence per £1 on the value of their estates. In Skye and the Hebrides the rate was almost fourteen pence. The Poor Law Board, under whose scrutiny the conditions in the Highlands now fell, saw the mass removal of a surplus population as providing the only answer to the problem. In 1857 Parliament encouraged this removal by the Emigration Advances Act, and in 1852 there was formed the Highlands and Islands Emigration Society. The best that chiefs could now do for their people was to make arrangements for emigrant ships to call, to take away into the refuge of exile the people who might have made their land sustain

A deserted cottage at Gruinard Bay, Wester Ross. *(Photo: Gordon Wright)*

them, but had never been allowed to hold enough of it to make success possible.

Except for a few scattered acts of resistance on South Uist, Barra and Benbecula, the deportees went quietly; and where a pathetic defiance was offered, the owners and their agents destroyed all shelter, and the law backed them up. The lack of resistance, unlike the behaviour of the Irish, was later admitted to be 'an important reason for official neglect'. Hugh Millar—labourer, geologist and theologian—summed up by writing 'the poor Highlander will shoot no one .... and so they will be left to perish'. There was no resistance because there was no notion in the Gaelic community of such a thing. The clan had deferred to its chiefs, had honoured them, followed them to death itself. They had never combined against their chiefs; the very concept was beyond them. Homesick, and emotionally scarred forever, they boarded the ships for Canada, and elsewhere, where they could re-create their glen, living off the land and using their own tongue.

But the Atlantic was wide, and the journey for most was for ever. The people who went, exploited, rejected and betrayed, suffered all the mental sorrows and physical hardships which their exile brought. The country from which they were evicted suffered too. Scotland lost half her heritage, and the desolation which then began has never found a remedy.

121

British Scotland

From around 1650 the dominant power in western Europe was France, and the Stewart kings were satellites of the French. The coming of king William—a Dutch patriot whose life's work was to obstruct French expansion and save the Netherlands—had carried England into the anti-French alliance. This foreign policy was continued by William's successors, and, as a result, wars with France were more or less constant from 1690 until 1815. At times British success was spectacular, especially in 1763 when Britain became a great imperial power, influential in Europe and in virtual control of North America and India.

These wars, as we have seen, had major economic consequences, encouraging the development of kelping in the Highlands, and textiles and iron-founding in various parts of Scotland. In commerce too, the growth of British colonial power offered many new opportunities which many Scots accepted. Men of wealth, investors and merchants, were first to seize these opportunities, but in time humbler persons found ways to benefit. Many went as colonists to farm on land of their own, to find careers in trades or professions, or to serve as agents for British trading interests in New York or Philadelphia, Madras or Bombay. Industries like cotton (and, later, jute) production, sugar-refining and tobacco-processing all developed, basing their increasing prosperity upon the raw materials of the British Empire. Many Scots even made careers in war itself, enlisting in Scottish regiments formed to fight Britain's battles wherever they might occur.

Few Scots therefore—except for the Jacobites—were feeling any sense of grievance as the eighteenth century proceeded. The intellectuals, lawyers and financiers of Edinburgh were enjoying that city's Golden Age; in Glasgow and the Clyde area, merchants, mill owners and ironmasters found little to complain about, and landowners saw their income from rentals rising. Britain was, in truth, an enormous success.

So at least it must have appeared to the small proportion of the population which made, or helped to make, the nation's decisions. In all Scotland only some 4-5000 people had the right to vote. In most counties there were only around thirty or so voters, and in the burghs, the Town Councils, themselves the creatures of the Merchant and Craft Guilds, chose the M.P.'s. This small group of the socially powerful and economically dominant, were well-pleased with their lot until things began to go wrong.

With the accession of George III in 1760 new political tensions arose over the king's methods and apparent purposes. His policies, which eventually brought about the American Revolution and the independence of Britain's thirteen American colonies by 1783, caused the gradual emergence of demands for political reforms; and the example of the independent United States, founded on freedom and equality for all its citizens, encouraged more and more people to support these demands.

Still, these successes and these grievances were all British in character. Between 1707 and the 1770's there was no voice speaking distinctively for Scotland; and indeed few signs that anything distinctively Scottish commanded any great interest or support, apart from the church, established by law, and satisfied with its privileged position.

Strangers to Scotland, and many Scots themselves, often feel puzzled by the hero-worship which so many bestow upon Robert Burns. The truth is that if Burns had never lived, Scotland could hardly have avoided going the way of ancient English-speaking kingdoms whose indentity is long lost, merged within a greater whole. Scotland today would rank along-side Mercia or Northumbria or Wessex, of interest as an antiquity, a curiosity or an affectation. If Scotland is anything more in modern times, it is because Burns, speaking as and for the ordinary man, stemmed the tide of history, flowing strongly in the direction of absorption and integration. His work meant that a sense of identity was preserved at a time when the politically active classes in Scotland showed little interest in any such sense. Aristocracy is by its nature international. It is ordinary people, involved with humbler local community life, who have greater national awareness. These ordinary people had no political power until more than a century had passed, but when in due course these people for whom Burns spoke did gain the right to political participation Scotland was still there.

Burns's lowly status and bucolic innocence have been greatly exaggerated, not least by himself, for what might be termed reasons of

Robert Burns by Alexander Nasmyth, 1787, 'detail' *(Scottish National Portrait Gallery)*

123

publicity. He was educated, beyond the average of his class and time, at an 'adventure' school, run by one Murdoch, as a business venture in Ayr. With this degree of education, and as the son of a tenant farmer, he had a modest measure of leisure, and an interest in the written word. Men like Burns, educated to full literacy and to some extent self-employed, were the most receptive audience for the political writings which attended the American Revolution, and, some ten years later, the French Revolution. Smiths and tailors, weavers and cobblers, were to some extent able to determine their own working hours, and could award themselves some time for study and discussion. Members of these crafts were famous for generations for their interest in radical politics, and around anvil and bench, loom and last, many an impromptu debating society flourished; discussing public events, recent publications and their own social condition. By the 1790's they could have been discussing the triumph of democracy in America and the principles of Liberty, Equality and Fraternity extended to all men by the French revolutionaries after 1789.

In England support for reform in the 1770's had led in time to the creation of the 'Friends of the People', mainly well-intentioned and high-minded nobles, gentry and urban professional men, whose friendship had in it elements of condescension. The Scottish 'Friends' were more genuinely 'of the People'. When in 1792 and in 1793 the Scottish 'Friends' assembled under the exciting influence of events in France, there were present representatives from active reform societies, mostly craftsmen and members of professions, from most areas of the country. Emerging as a

Thomas Muir of Huntershill. *(Sketch: David Martin)*

leading figure in the Convention was the young Glasgow lawyer, Thomas Muir, who had already gained a reputation by circulating pamphlets and analysing their contents at meetings of 'Friends' in many towns and villages. Unfortunately for Muir, the revolution in France had become increasingly violent in character. Sympathy for the revolution therefore ebbed; and the British government, genuinely afraid of revolutionary infection, and happy to see the reform movement discredited by bloodshed in France, now treated reform agitation as akin to treason, and prepared to act against reformers. Muir was the first victim of this policy; and, for circulating and encouraging the study of Tom Paine's *Rights of Man*, he was adjudged guilty of sedition and sentenced to be transported to Australia for fourteen years.

Once Britain was actually at war with France, after 1793, reformers were, inevitably, extremists, meeting in secret and frequently binding themselves by oaths—a practice always alarming to governments. There thus developed the 'United Scotsmen' (the title imitative of the already existing United Irishmen) organised in local branches and district committees, meeting clandestinely, members being known only by the name of the village, town or area branch which had sent them as delegates. One focus for activity in Angus, Perthshire and Fife, was Dundee, where several radical pamphlets were produced, an exploit which caused the Rev. Thomas Fysshe Palmer to be transported for seven years, and George Mealmaker, ringleader, organiser and author, for fourteen years. Mealmaker earned the grudging admiration of the authorities who were much surprised by the excellence of the writing of which this ordinary weaver was capable.

These stern measures had their effect; and though several conspiracy trials in Glasgow, and a major outbreak of violence at Tranent, showed that discontent simmered below the surface, the reformist cause undoubtedly weakened as the war dragged on. Burns contributed some poems which attracted the disapproval of authority. He had long ago written scathingly of the Hanoverians; and had attributed the Union, which had made of Scotland 'England's province', to 'hireling traitors .... such a parcel of rogues in a nation'. He now wrote encouragingly of the French Revolution, and contrasted the English indifference to liberty with the support felt for the cause in Scotland, in poems like *Ode on General Washington's Birthday* and *The Tree of Liberty*. He made in his mind a connection between the present struggle for liberty in France and the independence wars in Scottish history. His feelings prompted him to find new words to an old marching tune, reputedly played by Scots companies in the army of Joan of Arc. Using the tradition, reported by Barbour, that Bruce had delivered an inspirational address to his army at Bannockburn, Burns produced the poem, known by its opening words, *Scots wha hae*. By themselves these words are meaningless, and those who do not read or do not wish to listen, have been quick to find fault with the verses; but for others, the antiquity of the tune and the sentiments of Burns's words combine to provide Scotland with what ought to be her obvious and unchallenged National Anthem.

The interest of craftsmen in reform was not however purely intellectual or sentimental; they had very real practical grievances too. Between 1800 and 1808, for instance the income of handloom weavers had been halved, and their income continued to fall. In 1812 Glasgow weavers conducted a strike which lasted for nine weeks, an event which prompted the government and local powers in the city, to create a network of spies, informers and *agents provocateurs* to guard against any recurrence of such disturbing events.

In the aftermath of the war which ended in 1815, conditions of many workers worsened, and in both England and Scotland reformist agitation revived. In part men sought improvements in their wages and conditions, but more and more they were coming to the conclusion that only political power and friendly legislation could offer them reasonable future prospects. The United Scotsmen, back in the 1790's, had demanded votes for all men, votes by ballot, annual General Elections, and the payment of MP's; and these demands were the basis of the political agitation which grew during the immediate post-war years. A 'National Committee of Scottish Union Societies' had emerged during the 1812 strike. The word 'society' has a long pedigree in Scottish political history, Presbyterian extremists in the seventeenth century frequently being referred to as 'society men'. The Unions were territorial, not occupational; they were not *trade* unions, but area branches of the national organisation. In fact the National Committee and its organisation in the country gives every indication of being a revival of the United Scotsmen.

Events in England provided the spark which set in motion the events of 1819-20. The 'Manchester Massacre' or 'Peterloo' on 16 August 1819, provoked a storm of protests and demonstrations in Scotland. In Paisley cavalry had to be called in to disperse 5000 'Radicals', as the discontented were coming to be collectively called. A meeting in Stirling attracted 2000 people; in Airdrie a demonstration was led by a band playing *Scots Wha Hae*, for which action the entire band was arrested, and in Dundee a prominent reformer leader, the 'Radical Laird', Kinloch, was arrested for addressing a mass meeting on the Magdalen Green.

Irritated and alarmed by these and similar events, the government now acted, using the tried and true methods employed against the Covenanters in 1678, goading unknown numbers of an underground organisation into open defiance, thus rendering themselves open to identification and punishment. Thus, on 1 April 1820, Glasgow awoke to find, widely displayed around the city, posters in the name of a 'Committee .... for .... a Provisional Government', calling a general strike and promising armed action in support of the reformers' demands. Word was passed, without doubt by government agents, that supporters should march to Carron works where weapons would be found; and armies, source unknown, were reported to be mustering at Campsie and at Cathkin, under Kinloch and Marshal MacDonald, the French soldier of exiled Highland parentage. Encouraged at every step of the way by several mystery men bearing instructions and advice, an armed band, led by Andrew Hardie of the Castle Street Union, set off on 4 April to march from Glasgow to Carron pausing to collect reinforcements under John Baird, weaver and ex-soldier, at

Condorrat. Hardie had twenty-five men when he contacted Baird in the early hours of the 5th. Baird had only six men to add to the strength, but with this little force, Hardie and Baird proceeded towards Carron, only to be confronted by a cavalry force at Bonnymuir where the curiously well-informed authorities had ordered the Stirling military commander to meet the rebels. Nineteen 'rebels' were conveyed prisoners to Stirling Castle.

Meanwhile radicals at Strathaven had been instructed by messages from Glasgow, to march to Cathkin; and a force of twenty-five men, including the sixty-three-year-old James Wilson, veteran of the Friends of the People and, probably, of the United Scotsmen, marched as instructed. Warned of an ambush they returned home, but ten of them were sought, identified and arrested, and held in custody in Hamilton.

Rioters taken prisoner at Paisley were conveyed to jail in Greenock, where the good citizens attacked the Port Glasgow militia escorting the prisoners as they entered the town; attacked them again as they withdrew, and finally attacked the jail and released the prisoners.

So ended the 'Radical War'. On 30 August James Wilson was hanged and beheaded in Glasgow, and on 8 September Hardie and Baird were both hanged in Stirling. Other prisoners were transported to Australia, and hopes for reform seemed dashed for long years to come. The issue was kept alive in Parliament, where Lord Grey, once a member of the 'Friends of the People', had introduced a proposal for reform more or less annually, meeting as a rule nothing but ridicule. By 1830 however, the memories of the French revolution and its massacres and executions was fading, and the many absurdities of the unreformed political system were inviting mounting criticism. Thus, in 1830, the General Election saw the Whigs in power for the first time in fifty years; and Lord Grey, as Prime Minister, at long last carried his Reform Bill into law in 1832.

The Reform Act extended the vote to only a very small number of additional electors, but the frustrated lower orders persevered in their attempts to secure political rights, drafting the People's Charter —four of whose six points were the old demands of the United Scotsmen—and campaigning for ten years for its acceptance. Chartism was strong in Scotland, and Scots showed their historical awareness by giving to Chartist branches or clubs the names of Andrew Hardie, or John Baird, or James Wilson or Thomas Muir; and many clubs took to themselves the name of Robert Burns.

With the collapse in ridicule of the Chartist attempt in 1848, men at last seemed to despair of finding a solution to their material problems in gaining political power, and turned instead to the formation of Trade Unions, legalised since 1824, whose function was to negotiate with employers on wages and conditions, abandoning the apparently impossible dream of democracy.

There was logic in the change of tactic. The industrial developments of the preceding fifty years had been speeded up as war created demand for munitions encouraging investment in coal-mining and iron-founding. Industrial development was hardly possible without improvements in transportation. Raw material had to reach the factories, coal had to reach

The Union Canal at Edinburgh. *(Photo: Gordon Wright)*

the foundries, and the finished products had to reach distribution points en route to their various markets.

In the eighteenth century road construction had been undertaken under the supervision of such experts as Thomas Telford and John Macadam, but these roads—and the toll-financed Turnpike Roads provided by local counties and private landowners—did not really serve commercial purposes. For the transport of heavy and bulky cargoes the most economical means of transport was by water, on ship or barge. Thus the early expansion of heavy industry was assisted by the building of canals—the Monkland Canal, linking the Lanarkshire coal and ironfields with the wharves at Port Dundas in Glasgow; the Forth and Clyde Canal, crossing Scotland from Grangemouth to Bowling, and the Union Canal which connected industry in and around Edinburgh with the Forth and Clyde Canal at Bainsford, in Falkirk. These canals were effective, but goods moved very slowly. A faster method of distribution was found by adapting the technique, long-used in collieries, of having loaded wagons run on fixed rails from the point of production to the point of marketing. A railway of this sort had run from the Ayrshire coal-fields to Troon, where coal was shipped for Ireland, and similar wagon-ways existed in the Lothians. Along such lines horses could draw heavy loads, or stationary steam engines could, by rope or chain, draw wagons from point to point. With growing ingenuity in steam engineering came the production of locomotive engines, which themselves could run on the track provided, drawing trains of wagons behind them.

The pioneering work in steam engineering of James Watt was thus applied by George Stephenson; and in a remarkably short time railways were in operation, or under construction, throughout Britain. In Scotland, Edinburgh and Glasgow were linked by rail by 1842, and spur lines ran from the cities to the smaller towns in their areas. Railway connections with the south were established with the foundation in 1845 of the Caledonian Railway which linked Glasgow with the North Western Railway at Carlisle, and thence to London. In 1846 a similar plan linked the North British Railway, based in Edinburgh, with the English rail-head at Newcastle; while in 1850 a third link was provided when the Midland Railway, of Derby, connected with the Glasgow and South Western Railway at Dumfries.

Industrial costs were dramatically lowered and profits accordingly soared. Production of coal and iron (and steel) was in greatly increased demand and new jobs at all levels were provided—labourers to lay the tracks and civil engineers to plan them; mechanical engineers to design locomotives; labourers to smelt the iron-ore; platers and riveters to build them; drivers and firemen to crew the engines, and signalmen and surfacemen to see to the safe scheduled running of the trains.

The social consequences were also spectacular. The railway network integrated the country as never before, as travel was now possible for people with little leisure and no private transport. For the fortunate, railways made it possible to live at a distance from the place of employment, and suburbs arose around the cities, providing more work for architects, masons, builders, carpenters and slaters, plumbers and painters.

The outcome was a second, and vaster, Industrial Revolution. Soon the expansion of the railways was paralleled by the provision of steamships, and the firths of Clyde, Forth and Tay became highways of trade. Forth and Tay had long experience of this kind of thing, but for the Clyde it was something new. Glasgow's development had been retarded because the Clyde was not navigable for anything but small boats above Dumbarton. Glasgow merchants, even in the great days of the tobacco trade, had had to unload cargoes some twenty miles away; and, in order to avoid paying fees for the use of Greenock's harbours, these merchants had bought land and built their own port—Port Glasgow. In 1756 the Clyde just above Dumbarton was little more than a swamp, with a central channel of a mere fifteen inches in depth (less than half a metre). By engineering, begun by John Golborne in 1768, Glasgow's leading citizens began to deepen the channel, commissioning the building of walls and jetties, blasting heavy clay from the river bed, and employing a fleet of dredgers, until by 1886 they had a channel of some 20 feet deep (around 6 metres) and some 300 feet broad (100 metres). As has been said, 'Glasgow made the Clyde, and the Clyde made Glasgow'.

With a river now rendered navigable, Glasgow became one of the world's greatest centres for seaborne trade, and for the shipbuilding and marine engineering industries which provided the vessels. From the building at Port Glasgow in 1811 of Henry Bell's *Comet*, steamers provided the main means of access from Glasgow to all points on the Firth of Clyde, to the

The *Comet* near Port Glasgow. *(Photo: Glasgow Herald)*

Hebrides, to Ireland and England, and eventually to every continent in the world. The cousins, Robert and David Napier, pioneered in ship-building and engineering, and many who learned their skills in Napier's yards became major figures in the world of shipping themselves, as builders, engineers or as operators of fleets of steamers. These steamers carried locomotives from Springburn and St. Rollox to India, Africa and South America; metalware from Glasgow itself, from Lanarkshire and Falkirk; fabrics from Paisley and the Vale of Leven to all corners of the globe. 'Clyde-built' was taken to be an indicator of excellence, and Glasgow especially, and central Scotland as a whole, became one of the busiest and most thriving corners of the 'workshop of the world' which Victorian Britain had become.

For all this success a heavy price was paid by the people whose labour made it all happen. Work in 'heavy' industries and in textile production was unhealthy and often dangerous for the men, women and children who worked long hours for miserably low wages. Even away from their work the workers could not escape from the consequences of industrialisation. Their homes, often built by the employers conveniently close to the place of employment, were all too commonly slums; over-crowded, insanitary and polluted by smoke and fumes from factories and railway yards. Employers, most of them of humble social origins themselves, were generally harsh and

130

ruthless, feeling no obligation towards those less successful than themselves. Most saw their success as proof of their own superior qualities, and found justification in economic and religious theories for their readiness to accept the gross extremes of wealth and poverty. It is a major tragedy that when Scotland did once prosper, all but a handful of her people derived no benefit from that prosperity.

Such social responsibility as there was, had come from the church. For many generations education and relief of poverty had been administered by the church. This system had worked acceptably while most of the people were Presbyterian churchgoers; but by the mid-nineteenth century the church had lost most of its contacts with industrial workers living in the worst city areas and tended increasingly to be an organisation concerned wholly with 'respectable' people. Also, immigrants from Ireland, brought over by employers to work in mines, on railway construction and other heavy and unattractive jobs, had brought with them their Catholic faith. Thus, whereas in 1755 there were no Catholics in Ayrshire, 2 in Lanarkshire, 3 in Renfrewshire, none in Dumbartonshire and 8 in Stirlingshire, by the late 1800's these industrialised counties had a large and growing Catholic population. To make the Church of Scotland responsible for the social care of these new communities was hardly realistic.

To make matters worse, in 1843, after long years of controversy over the right of the state to interfere in church affairs, a substantial proportion of the ministers, elders and members left the Church of Scotland and founded the Free Church. This Disruption had far-reaching consequences. The Free Church set itself the task of providing a second network of churches, manses and schools, duplicating those of the established 'Auld Kirk'. The latter, weakened by the loss of almost half its members, was no longer able to meet its traditional responsibilities, and thus the provision of poor relief and of education at parish level became a matter for the state or the local authorities in counties and burghs.

Parliament had acted at various times during the century to remedy some of the worst consequences of industrialisation. A succession of Factory Acts had regulated hours and age of workers, and the Coal Mines Acts had prohibited underground working by women and children. But the issues of politics were still dictated by the interest and opinions of a minority. Despite the extension of voting rights in 1832, 1867 and 1884, only 58 per cent of adult males had the vote, and women not at all. Political battles were fought over the issues which interested the comparatively prosperous, comparatively secure sections of the community.

Unemployment was not an issue because few voters were unemployed. Housing conditions were not an issue because voters were, in general, comfortably housed. Poverty could be blamed on laziness and drink, because voters were seldom poor. Politics, as the century neared its end, were dominated by Irish Home Rule, the recurring massacres of Armenians and Bulgarians by Turks, and the proposal to abandon Free Trade and re-introduce protective tariffs.

For the problems of the industrial workers and the poor to secure attention a change in the whole basis of politics and parties was required.

To Be or Not To Be

By 1914 some 65 per cent of Scotland's people lived in the central belt of the country between the Firth of Forth and Clyde, and a steady drift from the countryside into towns and cities continued, until, by the 1950's, 80 per cent of Scots were concentrated in this area. The major employers were the 'heavy' industries—coal mining, iron and steel-founding, shipbuilding and engineering. More than 200,000 families derived their livelihood from these industries, and a further 150,000 were sustained by employment in textile production. Thus more than half the population was dependent upon labour-intensive manufacturing industry.

In the late 1800's and into the twentieth century, these industries were earning large profits, and great wealth came to the owners, who enjoyed, in late Victorian and Edwardian times, life-styles enviable for leisure and luxury. Unfortunately, though individual acts of charity were frequent, there was no official social conscience; and, in the presence of great riches, industrial workers lived lives governed by low wages, long hours and frequently unhealthy and dangerous working conditions. Away from the workplace, living conditions were, as came to be realised, a national disgrace. Housing, whether provided by employers or by builders planning to draw rents, was generally cheap in construction, poor in quality and grudging in space. If employers had provided high-quality housing, then their profits would have suffered. If builders had offered high quality rented homes, a low-paid workforce could never have paid the rents required. So, buildings were crammed into confined sites, often cheek-by-jowl with colliery and yard, factory and foundry; rooms were small, and around 53 per cent of families, no matter how numerous, lived in houses with one or two rooms. Indoor sanitation was absent or shared, and the effect of these conditions upon the health and life-expectancy of the people was bound to be damaging. Typhoid fever and even cholera survived into the twentieth century; epidemics of diphtheria and scarlet fever were virtually annual, and tuberculosis killed thousands. Poverty led to malnutrition, and diseases caused by diet deficiency, like rickets, were common. To make matters worse, the houses were themselves aging, and new building was quite inadequate to provide homes for the rising population between 1850 and 1900.

To make matters worse, though few could have realised it, Scotland's days of industrial success were already numbered. The appearance of economic success endured and examples of technological excellence (such as the building of the first turbine-powered steamer, *King Edward* in 1901) occurred, but the basis of Scotland's role as one of the world's workshops was weakening.

The resources of iron and coal upon which industrial growth had been

The *King Edward* sailing on the River Clyde. *(Photo: G. E. Langmuir)*

founded, had been, or were becoming, exhausted. Many countries were able to exploit resources far beyond those available in Scotland, and were also better placed geographically to manufacture and trade. These emerging competitors commonly employed modern technology, having learned from and improved upon Scottish—and English—exemplars. Scotland's industrial experience proved the truth of Andrew Carnegie's remark that 'pioneering don't pay'.

To a great extent, therefore, decline arose from realities of mineralogy geology and geography, for which no one can be blamed. Criticism can, however, be made of the owners and managers who persevered with old-fashioned equipment and methods, preferring unbroken production in the present to the prospect of greater productivity in the future.

Also, as had been the case in the 1700's, men who met with economic success in their chosen field tended to reward themselves by abandoning that field and adopting instead the life-style of leisured aristocrats. In Scotland's industrial heyday her industries were planned and operated by men who were technically expert, or, at least, well-informed. Men like Lord Kelvin could spend mornings researching and lecturing on the theories of physics and engineering, and the afternoons in the engineering shop, applying these theories to the practical task of production. But as time passed, owners became remote, mere investors or administrators, detached from technological experience or experiment. The managers to whom they left the day-to-day running of industry, all too often showed the practical man's contempt for theory—'mere' theory as the revealing phrase puts it. The close integration of theory and practice characteristic of the rise of Scottish industry—the tradition of James Watt and Lord Kelvin, and of Robert and David Napier, the virtual creators of the Clyde's greatness as a centre of shipbuilding and marine engineering—gradually disappeared.

This industrial decline was not, of course, clearly apparent at the time. Only in later years when statistics became available did it emerge that Scottish heavy industries reached, in 1913, a peak of production never to be achieved again. The decline was halted, temporarily, by the boost to productivity given by the Great War, but by the 1920's Scotland was distinguished by persistently high rates of unemployment and similarly high rates of emigration. The population was static and aging, and, in the post war world, the Scottish economy was clearly sick and failing.

Inevitably these developments had political consequences. Scotland was usually overwhelmingly loyal at election times to the Liberal party. That party was supported by employers and workers alike in industrial areas, while in the rural constituencies and in the Highlands, the influence of the Free Church, often victimised by Tory landowners, was exerted in the Liberal interest.

Towards the end of the century however, things began to change. The Liberal commitment to Home Rule for Ireland led to a split in the party, and to the formation of the Liberal-Unionists. This group—still Liberal in terms of economic theory—draw support from Protestant industrialists, business-men and others of the middle-class, unwilling to support any diminution of British sovereignty and hostile to the placing of Ireland's Protestant minority under an all-Irish and, therefore, overwhelmingly Catholic parliament in Dublin. As a result the number of Liberal seats in Scotland fell from fifty-seven in 1885 to thirty-nine in 1886. The Conservatives, who won only ten in 1885, won twelve in 1886, and enjoyed the support of sixteen Liberal Unionists.

As more working men joined the electorate, and as new issues like high tariffs and the threat of more expensive food arose, Liberal strength momentarily revived, and in the elections between 1906 and 1910 the Liberals enjoyed something like their old dominance. Events during and immediately after the war, however, disrupted the Liberals who suffered a fatally damaging split into rival factions. At the same time the ordinary voters, seeking political action to fulfil their hopes and remedy their grievances, began to turn to the Labour Party.

The basic idea, that working people ought to have, and to support, a party which was specifically theirs, preoccupied with issues relevant to them, was as old as the Chartists of the 1830's and 1840's. The idea revived in the 1880's in Scotland, with the formation of the Scottish Labour Party. This venture did not long survive the departure of its moving spirit, James Keir Hardie, to England, where, in 1893 Hardie and others formed the Independent Labour Party. This party, combining with some socialist societies, and with the support of a number of Trade Unions, formed firstly, the Labour Representation Committee, and then the Labour Party. This new party won two Scottish seats in the General Election of 1906. Its strength remained modest, seven seats being won in 1918; but in 1922, as the Liberals destroyed themselves by internal feuding, Scotland saw the election of thirty Labour members (to the Liberals' sixteen, Liberal Unionists' twelve and Conservatives' fifteen). The Liberals rallied briefly in 1923, but thereafter the Labour Party became the preferred refuge of anti-Conservative voters.

The M.P's elected in 1922, characterised as the 'Red Clydesiders' in the press were, in these early days, an impressive contingent, representative of working class aspirations not only to power, but to dignity and culture and

John MacLean. *(Photo: Glasgow Herald)*   James Maxton. *(Photo: Glasgow Herald)*

respect, which had been growing for thirty years and more. Men like John Wheatley and Tom Johnstone were to prove themselves in Cabinet office. James Maxton, though never holding any executive responsibility, was throughout his career a loved and admired orator and tribune of the people. George Buchanan had a political career long enough to allow him to make a valuable contribution to the 'Welfare State' legislation of 1945-50. Not all important figures were in Parliament or enjoyed successful political careers. One man, seen by later generations as deserving of the greatest respect, was John MacLean, a Glasgow school-teacher who taught and preached the values and merits of socialism, suffering imprisonment and persecution culminating in his premature death.

Such men were the main personalities in Scottish politics in the years of industrial strife and political change which followed the war.

Strikes in the coal-fields in the 1920's had brought great suffering and apparent defeat to the miners, fighting against attempts to worsen their conditions of employment. In 1926 the miners took the lead in the General Strike, and persevered in their resistance for a year after their allies in other unions had given up.

It was difficult to maintain the rights and interests of industrial workers as post-war unemployment mounted, culminating in the experiences of the Depression which struck in 1929. Hardest hit were the industries upon which Scotland especially depended—shipbuilding and engineering, for whose products there was now no world market. Demand for coal and steel thus fell, and as workers thrown idle struggled to live within their means, demand for furnishings, household goods, clothing and similar products fell also, and the whole population was caught in a web of poverty and fear of poverty.

The Labour government which had taken office, with Liberal support, in

1929, could not agree upon a policy to meet the crisis. Its leaders co-operated in the formation of a 'National Government' supposedly all-party but in reality dominated by Conservatives, in 1931. In that year a General Election gave that government a huge majority, as voters turned in panic to the methods, financial policies and presumed expertise of the Conservatives. In Scotland fifty-eight supporters of the National Government were elected, with only eight Liberals and seven Labour members surviving in opposition.

Despite this apparent collapse, the Labour Party in the long run benefited from the events which followed. Relief payments, given as unemployment insurance benefit for some weeks, and then as 'National Assistance' or 'dole', were ungenerous and grudging; and dole payments were attended by harsh and humiliating surveillance as the 'Means Test' was applied, with inspectors empowered to enter homes and pry into the circumstances (and even the cooking pots) of the unemployed to ensure that their dependence upon relief was genuine and total. So, though the Depression had, initially, driven voters into the arms of the Conservatives, the memory of the 'Means Test' became a great national folk-myth from which the Labour Party was ever afterwards able to draw advantage. A determination never to return to the conditions of the '30's, and never to permit mass unemployment, was fundamental to Labour's policies until the 1970's.

The National Government did take measures to revive the economy. Regions of severe unemployment were designated 'Special Areas', and industrial estates, producing such items as clocks and electrical goods were established in places like the Vale of Leven, Hillington near Glasgow, and in Dundee. Symbolic of the government's willingness to use state funds to revive industry, was the provision of finance to enable work to restart upon the great new Cunard liner, begun in 1930, which had lain rusting at Clydebank since 1931. In 1933 work began again on this vessel, Yard number 534, which was launched in September 1934 as the *Queen Mary*.

Launching of the *Queen Mary* at Clydebank. *(Photo: Glasgow Herald)*

136

Despite these efforts, the new industries came nowhere near to absorbing the numbers of unemployed workers, and only the approach of war and the rearmament programme, which revived the heavy industries, ended the years of idleness.

Scottish factories, yards and foundries made a massive contribution to the British war effort, while the Clyde estuary became the major anchorage for merchant ships arriving in convoys, bringing food, materials and troops from around the world, especially from America and Canada.

Britain's capacity to survive depended upon the Atlantic routes being kept open, and Greenock was strategically placed to shelter and service warships and merchant ships engaged in the Battle of the Atlantic. Though Scotland as a whole never came under sustained attack from the air, sharp attacks in March and May, 1941, virtually destroyed Clydebank and inflicted heavy damage and casualties upon Greenock.

The waging of modern war had brought the people under closer government control than ever before. Conscription and direction of labour, the organising of civil defence services, and rationing of food and clothing, all entailed centralised decision-making and centralised administration. The experience of wartime merely rounded off a tendency towards centralisation and a gradual diminishing of local distinctions which had been progressing throughout the century. More aspects of life were seen as being 'the government's business', and were subject to parliamentary decision and legislation—pensions, insurance arrangements, housing standards for instance. Technology had made such changes in communications that communities, which for centuries had lived a unique life of their own, now were linked with distant places by road, rail and sometimes air; their people read the same newspapers with the same news and the same advertisements as were read by people several hundred miles away; they listened to the same radio broadcasts, and viewed the same films, and they could pursue social or economic discussions over the telephone. In all these ways the people of Scotland were being influenced into feeling an identity not only of interest, but of personality, with all other parts of Britain. Labour's nationalisation programme after 1945 centralised control of transport and major industries in London, where the headquarters of banks and private industries already tended to be.

Both major parties governed on the assumption that Britain was, and ought to be, a centralised unitary state; and both played down, for their different reasons, any lingering notion that Scotland had any special identity in the modern world. For Conservatives, *Britain* commanded patriotic loyalty, while the Labour party thought in terms of class rather than nation. Labour had once shared the old Liberal commitment to Home Rule, but, after 1945, Mr Attlee, the Labour Prime Minister, explained that since Scots now enjoyed a Labour government they had no need for Home Rule, and the commitment was abandoned.

Political support for Home Rule had existed after a fashion ever since the 1790's. As the 1800's proceeded, the Liberal Party and early Labour pioneers were pledged to Home Rule. Pressure groups grew and withered, but by 1920 there was ample reason to assume that, with the Liberal Party

The Duke of Montrose, Compton Mackenzie, R. B. Cunningham Graham, Christopher Murray Grieve, James Valentine and John MacCormick at the first public meeting of the National Party of Scotland, St. Andrews Halls, Glasgow, 1928. *(Photo: Glasgow Herald)*

in ruins and Ireland in revolt, Scottish Home Rule was a mere dream.

Then in August 1922, there appeared *The Scottish Chapbook*, in which the young poet Christopher Murray Grieve demanded that Scots writers should begin to 'speak with our own voice for our own times'. They should engage in a serious examination of profound themes seen through Scottish eyes. Thanks to Grieve—or 'Hugh MacDiarmid' as he called himself—and a generation or more of men and women inspired by his example, Scottish writing ceased to be provincial and trivial as it had become for some fifty preceding years, becoming rather the source of a new national intellectual reawakening, reminiscent of the days of the Enlightenment. What followed might be unfamiliar by English standards, but in Europe and Ireland a cultural revival followed by political action was a familiar experience.

Several organisations favouring Home Rule functioned in the 1920's. The Home Rule Association had indeed been formed in the 1890's; and it was now joined in its work by the Scots National Movement and the Scots National League. The former was profoundly influenced by cultural developments, while the latter was more anxious to get on with the work of building up a force which could challenge the existing political parties at election time. Just as the Labour Party emerged when enough people saw the need for a class to have a party of its own, so now the League based its appeal on the need for a nation to regain the power to devise policies and arrange priorities in the best interests of the people of that nation. These and other groups combined in 1928 (following upon the rejection of a Home Rule Bill in Parliament in 1927), to form the National Party of Scotland; and later, after another accession of support, the Scottish National Party.

The new party, after some initial doubts, followed the strategy line of the Scots National League, and proceeded to challenge the established parties at the polls, with results varying from the ridiculous to the reasonably encouraging. The war was a setback for a party trying to capture public attention, and the party's prospects were not improved when a powerful faction abandoned the policy of election-fighting, and adopted instead the older tactic of seeking to influence existing parties to adopt measures which tended towards eventual self-government, at least on all matters of domestic policy.

This breakaway group and its leader John M. MacCormick, a founder and long-time secretary of the Scottish National Party, met with considerable success in the late 1940's and early 1950's. They organised a series of annual National Assemblies, and produced the 'Scottish Covenant' inviting signatures of support from all who would pledge themselves to place Home Rule above partisan loyalties. Some two million signatures were secured, but the Covenant Association had no means of compelling politicians to respond to moral pressures. The politicians, with cold cynicism, responded that only votes cast at General Elections were acceptable as indicators of the electorate's wishes. The initiative on the Nationalist side was thus restored to the SNP which had remained committed to the election process. They had indeed enjoyed their one success when in April 1945, at a by-election in Motherwell, Dr Robert D. McIntyre became the first ever Scottish Nationalist MP.

Dr. Robert MacIntyre, the first SNP MP. *(Photo: Gordon Wright)*

The post-war years were bleak for the SNP, as the Covenant commanded attention from friendly countrymen, and when party political loyalties for most took precedence over national sentiments. But gradually political developments began to play into Nationalist hands.

The Labour government of 1945 became unpopular surprisingly quickly. Though the feared post-war unemployment did not materialise, voters were indignant at the years of hardship and 'austerity' which had followed the war, instead of the joyous comfort which many had thought would come with victory. Surviving the 1950 General Election by the skin of its teeth, the Labour government fell at the next hurdle, the election of 1951. There followed thirteen years of Conservative government, and Conservative support in England rose steadily at the elections of 1955 and 1959. In Scotland however, the Conservatives reached a peak of success in 1955, winning thirty-six seats to Labour's thirty-four, but declining fairly rapidly in subsequent elections. Scottish voters were in fact beginning to behave in a very different fashion from their English counterparts.

The reasons for this divergence lay in the economic policies pursued by the Conservatives and their consequences. As the government sought to free the economy from the constraints which Labour had seen fit to impose upon it, there were recurring crises as the economy around London expanded rapidly and inflation threatened. At such times the Treasury would impose restrictions, growth would slow down and inflationary pressure would ease and all was then thought to be well. But in Scotland, growth had hardly begun when restrictions were imposed, and increasingly it seemed to many that one policy did not really meet the needs of different parts of Britain. Also, to an increasing extent Scottish factories were branches of English firms. When times were hard and these firms felt the need to economise they would close their branches and draw back towards their centre. The result for Scotland was recurring outbreaks of unemployment and feelings of injustice and discrimination.

Reading the political signs and responding to the decline in their support, the Conservatives by 1960 had begun to try to placate Scottish opinion by abandoning their insistence upon one single policy for all, and instead extending special favours to Scotland. The car industry, lost to Scotland since the early 1900's, was virtually directed by government pressure and incentives, to Linwood. A road bridge over the Forth, long dismissed as an idle dream, became a reality, and a Tay road bridge was also sanctioned. All was politically too little too late however, and Scottish voters gave decisive support to Labour in 1964 and 1966 when Scotland returned forty-three and then forty-six Labour members to the Conservatives' twenty-four and twenty.

In 1966 Scottish voters clearly trusted Labour to extend prosperity to Scotland, and their disappointment was intense when the new Labour government promptly faced yet another economic crisis, which they sought to meet by using the same methods as those employed by the Conservatives. At this moment of maximum disillusion with both political parties a by-election was called in Hamilton. This was seen as a safe Labour seat. It had been held for Labour even in the disaster of 1931, but now, in 1967, it was won by Mrs Winifred Ewing of the Scottish National Party with a majority of 1799.

It was widely remarked after this event, that Scottish politics would never be the same again. Political parties, television companies and newspaper owners all fell over themselves to show interest in, and concern for, Scottish sensitivities and ambitions. It was all rather hectic, and it didn't last. In 1970, though Scotland supported Labour loyally, and Mrs Ewing lost her seat, a Conservative revival in England brought them a victory which few had expected or predicted. The SNP suffered a set back in its progress, but it managed to keep a parliamentary presence with the election of Donald Stewart in the Western Isles constituency.

At this point fate took a hand, and the SNP enjoyed a dramatic upturn in its fortunes. The argument against the SNP put forward on doorsteps by Labour and Conservative canvassers was essentially that Scotland was too small, too poor and too inexperienced for its people ever to contemplate independence. The Scottish voters had obviously agreed with this assessment. But in 1970 oil companies prospecting in the North Sea found reserves of first gas and then oil. Oil in modern times has an almost magic quality, linked as it is in the public imagination with the spectacular wealth of American tycoons and Arab potentates. The oil was admittedly on the continental shelf in international waters, but it was in a sector allocated by international agreement to Britain, and it was nearer to Scotland than to anywhere else. The SNP gleefully proclaimed 'It's Scotland's Oil', and Britain's politicians found that Scotland could not be made to seem too poor for independence any more. They did their best. They argued that the oil belonged to the oil companies and not to Scotland, ignoring the real point which was not ownership but the right to tax and draw royalties. They argued that there was only a tiny amount of oil, and that silly Scots were getting excited about nothing, but time proved that that argument was erroneous. Becoming subtler they then appealed to the Scots' better nature, encouraging them to feel ashamed and greedy if they were to persevere in their claim to the oil. The SNP meantime hammered away on the theme of the marvellous things which could be done for the Scottish economy and society with the revenues from the industry.

In 1972 and 1973 the SNP came close to victory in by-elections in Stirling and Dundee East before winning another in Govan. In February 1974 seven Nationalist members were returned at the General Election, and when later that year the minority Labour government sought a safer mandate to govern, the Nationalist contingent rose to eleven.

That election was crucial, and though many Nationalists were delighted with their progress, their success was more apparent than real. The Labour Party had managed to retain its seats in Scotland, though they had to promise a Scottish parliament and in other respects steal the Nationalists' thunder. Between 1974 and 1979 the SNP was out-manoeuvred as parliamentary experts dragged out interminable discussions on the Labour plan for a Scottish Assembly. The SNP helped in their own downfall by innocently acting as though the fight was won, and they could enjoy the luxury of ceasing to make greedy noises about oil, and turn instead to talk of

Douglas Crawford, George Reid, Gordon Wilson, Douglas Henderson, Winifred Ewing, Donald Stewart, Margaret Bain, Hamish Watt, Ian MacCormick, Andrew Welsh and George Thomson, the eleven SNP MPs elected in 1974. *(Photo: Gordon Wright)*

problems such as the plight of single-parent families.

Meanwhile the Labour leadership found that they could not command the voting loyalty of a number of their English members. The Bill to grant Scotland an Assembly was firstly, made to be subject to a referendum, and then a requirement was added that the Bill would become effective only if 40 per cent of the total Scottish electorate supported it in the referendum. Labour and Conservative opponents combined to fight for a 'No' vote in the referendum, and as time dragged on the Scottish voters became increasingly bored with the whole business. In any case the Labour government was becoming increasingly unpopular, and the Bill suffered in popularity as a result. When the referendum was eventually held in March 1979 it was supported by a majority, but not by 40 per cent of the electorate.

Prime Minister Callaghan was caught between the SNP members, whose votes were necessary for the survival of his government, and a number of his own members who refused to allow the Scotland Act to be accepted. The Nationalists then threatened that unless the government would see the Bill through the Commons they would support a vote of no confidence in Callaghan. Just as in 1707 an attempt at political blackmail went wrong, so now in 1979 the SNP, acting on the most righteous principle, voted with the Conservatives, and the Labour government fell.

At the General Election which followed, the Conservatives were returned to power, which they have enjoyed ever since. But the SNP paid a bitter price for their purity of principle. In 1979 they returned only two of their eleven members, Donald Stewart in the Western Isles and Gordon Wilson in Dundee East. In 1983 again they held only these two seats, while in 1987 they lost these two, winning three others by way of compensation.

Meanwhile Labour in Scotland went from strength to strength, securing fifty of the seventy-one seats in 1987 to the Conservatives' eleven. The Conservative government, and particularly the Prime Minister, Mrs Thatcher, arouse in Scotland a most profound antagonism, and Labour enjoys an easy dominance in consequence.

But Labour has had to pay a price for its success. It has been driven by the logic of events further and further into a Nationalist stance. Though Labour's official policy remains firmly Unionist, it has had to give the firmest possible commitment to a Scottish Assembly. A substantial number of Labour MP's have also come to feel that if Scotland remains British it will be governed for the foreseeable future by Prime Minister Thatcher whom they so deeply detest and that Scotland will escape from Conservative rule only if it escapes from English rule.

The SNP meantime, showing much more political sophistication than in 1979, has campaigned steadily on the need for independence as the only way in which the clear will of the Scottish electorate can be democratically implemented. The absurdity of a political system which places Scotland under the control, and subject to the policies, of a party which cannot muster enough Scottish members to man the Scottish Office and relevant parliamentary committees, has become more and more widely appreciated. The SNP also has moved to counter the damaging, albeit cynical, tag of 'separatist' by talking of 'Independence in Europe', thus showing a mature awareness of realities as well as indicating a readiness to participate in and co-operate with the wider world. In 1988 the SNP, in the person of Jim Sillars, won a by-election, in Govan once more, on the 'Independence in Europe' platform. His success revived interest in the Home Rule issue.

A 'Campaign for a Scottish Assembly', formed mainly by supporters of Home Rule, who for one reason or another would not join the SNP, had been operating without arousing any marked interest, but now, under its auspices, a Scottish Constitutional Convention, to which all political parties and most public bodies had been invited to send representatives, would try to produce proposals for a measure of self-government which might command support of the majority of the Scottish people. The Conservative Party refused to participate; the SNP, resenting Labour domination, distrusting Labour's good faith, and smarting from the bitter experience of 1979, participated until it became clear that others in the Convention would not agree to place independence as an option to the Scottish people, and then ended that participation.

It now remains to be seen whether Labour and Liberal Democrats can combine to produce some agreed plan from the Convention, and whether they can devise some means of persuading a United Kingdom government and Parliament to allow any such plan to be implemented.

If they succeed, some measure of self-government may follow. If they fail, Labour may seek to preserve its ascendancy in Scotland by adopting a fully Nationalist stance, claiming the right to govern Scotland by virtue of its majority in that country. Failing such action, the SNP will persevere in its attempt to whittle away at Labour strength until they achieve a decisive number of Scottish seats.

In either event, the 'auld sang', which ended in 1707, may yet be heard once again.

Scotland: Population

1801	1,608,420
1811	1,805,864
1821	2,091,521
1831	2,364,386
1841	2,620,184
1851	2,888,742
1861	3,062,294
1871	3,360,018
1881	3,735,573
1891	4,025,647
1901	4,472,103
1911	4,760,904
1921	4,882,497
1931	4,842,980
1941	No Census
1951	5,095,969
1961	5,179,000
1971	5,229,000
1981	5,130,000
1988	5,094,000

Scottish General Election Results

	Others	Labour ILP Co-op	Liberal	Lib. Unionist National Lib.	Conservative
1868			52		8
1874			40		20
1880			53		7
1885	Crofter: 5		57		10
1886	Crofter: 5		39	16	12
1892	Crofter: 5		45	12	10
1895			39	14	19
1900			34	17	21
1906		2	58	4	8
1910		2	59	3	8
1910		3	58	4	7
1918		7	34		32
1922	Comm.: 1	29	16	12	15
1923		34	23		16
1924	Comm.: 1	26	9		37
1929		37	14		22
1931		7	8	8	50
1935	Comm.: 1	24	3	8	37
1945	Comm.: 1	40	0	5	25
1950		37	2	6	26
1951		35	1	6	29
1955		34	1	6	30
1959		38	1	6	26
1964		43	4		24
1966		46	5		20
1970	SNP: 1	44	3		23
1974	SNP: 7	40	3		21
1974	SNP: 11	41	3		16
1979	SNP: 2	44	3		22
1983	SNP: 2	41	7		21
1987	SNP: 3	50	7		11

Scottish Contacts

THE COLLEGE OF PIPING & THE PIOBAIREACHD SOCIETY
16-24 Otago St. Glasgow G12 8JH. Tel: 041-334 3587.

ROYAL SCOTTISH PIPE BAND ASSOCIATION
45 Washington St. Glasgow G3 8AZ. Tel: 041-221 5414.

THE CLARSACH SOCIETY
87 Swanston Ave. Edinburgh EH10 7DA. Tel: 031-445 2022.

NATIONAL ASSOCIATION OF ACCORDION & FIDDLE CLUBS
Abbey House,Culross KY12 8JB. Tel: 0383-880081.

TRADITIONAL MUSIC & SONG ASSOCIATION OF SCOTLAND
10 Belmont St. Aberdeen AB1 1JE. Tel: 0224-632978.

NATIONAL LIBRARY OF SCOTLAND
George IV Bridge, Edinburgh EH1 1EW. Tel: 031-226 4531.

BOOK TRUST SCOTLAND
15a Lynedoch St. Glasgow G3 6EF. Tel: 041-332 0391.

AN COMUNN LEABHRAICHEAN (The Gaelic Books Council)
Dept. of Celtic, University of Glasgow G20 7EL. Tel: 041-330 5190

AN COMUNN GAIDHEALACH (The Highland Association)
109 Church St. Inverness. Tel: 0463-231226.

THE SCOTS LANGUAGE SOCIETY
The Sandeman Library, Kinnoull St. Perth.

SCOTTISH POETRY LIBRARY
Tweeddale Court, 14 High St., Edinburgh EH1 1TE. Tel: 031-557 2876

SCOTTISH FOLK ARTS GROUP
49 Blackfriars St. Edinburgh EH1 1NB. Tel: 031-557 3090.

SCOTTISH PUBLISHERS ASSOCIATION
25a S W Thistle St Lane, Edinburgh EH2 1EW. Tel: 031-225 5795.

THE BUCHAN HERITAGE SOCIETY
12 Laburnum Grove, Peterhead AB4 6GA. Tel: 0779-73738.

THE SCOTTISH ARTS COUNCIL
12 Manor Pl. Edinburgh EH3 7DD. Tel: 031-226 6051.

THE ROYAL SCOTTISH COUNTRY DANCE SOCIETY
12 Coates Cres. Edinburgh EH3 7AF. Tel: 031-225 3854.

SCOTTISH OFFICIAL BOARD OF HIGHLAND DANCE
32 Grange Loan, Edinburgh EH9 2NR. Tel: 031-668 3965.

SCOTTISH WILDLIFE TRUST
25 Johnston Terr. Edinburgh EH1 2NH. Tel: 031-226 4602.

NATURE CONSERVANCY COUNCIL
12 Hope Terr. Edinburgh EH9 2AS. Tel: 031-447 4784.

THE SALTIRE SOCIETY
9 Fountain Close, High St. Edinburgh EH1 1TF. Tel: 031-556 1836.

THE ST ANDREW SOCIETY
PO Box 84, Edinburgh. Tel: 031-228 1902.

ROYAL SCOTTISH ACADEMY OF MUSIC AND DRAMA
100 Renfrew St. Glasgow G2 3DB. Tel: 041-332 4101.

THE NATIONAL TRUST FOR SCOTLAND
5 Charlotte Sq. Edinburgh EH2 4DU. Tel: 031-226 5922.

SCOTTISH TOURIST BOARD
20 Ravelston Terr. Edinburgh EH4 3EU. Tel: 031-332 2433.

SCOTCH WHISKY ASSOCIATION
20 Atholl Cres. Edinburgh EH3 8HF. Tel: 031-229 4383.

SCOTTISH FILM COUNCIL
Dowanhill, 74 Victoria Cres. Rd. Glasgow G12 9JN. Tel: 041-334 9314.

SCOTTISH RECORD OFFICE
HM General Register House, Princes St. Edinburgh EH1 3YY.
Tel: 031-556 6585.

HISTORIC BUILDINGS AND MONUMENTS
20 Brandon St. Edinburgh EH3 5RA. Tel: 031-244 3107.

NATIONAL MUSEUMS OF SCOTLAND
Chambers St. Edinburgh EH1. Tel: 031-225 7534.

SCHOOL OF SCOTTISH STUDIES
27 George Sq. Edinburgh EH8 9LD. Tel: 031-667 1011.

SCOTTISH TARTANS SOCIETY
Scottish Tartans Museum, Drummond St. Comrie PH6 2DW.
Tel: 0764-70779.

SCOTS ANCESTRY RESEARCH SOCIETY
3 Albany St. Edinburgh EH1 3PY. Tel: 031-556 4220.

SCOTTISH HISTORY SOCIETY
Dept. of Scottish History, University of St Andrews KY16 9AJ.

Index

150

Flower of Scotland

Oh flower of Scotland,
When will we see your like again,
That fought and died for,
Your wee bit hill and glen
And stood against him
Proud Edward's army
And sent him homeward,
To think again.

The hills are bare now,
And autumn leaves lie thick and still,
O'er land that is lost now,
Which those so dearly held
That stood against him
Proud Edward's army
And sent him howeward,
To think again.

Those days are passed now,
And in the past they must remain,
But we can still rise now
And be the nation again
That stood against him
Proud Edward's army
And sent him homeward,
To think again.

Words and Music: Roy Williamson.

Scots Wha Hae

Scots, wha hae wi Wallace bled,
Scots, wham Bruce has aften led,
Welcome to your gory bed,
Or to victorie!

Now's the day, and now's the hour;
See the front o' battle lour;
See approach proud Edward's power—
Chains and slaverie!

Wha will be a traitor-knave?
Wha can fill a coward's grave?
Wha sae base as be a slave?
Let him turn and flee!

Wha for Scotland's king and law
Freedom's sword will strongly draw,
Freeman stand, or freeman fa',
Let him follow me!

By oppression's woes and pains!
By your sons in servile chains!
We will drain our dearest veins,
But they *shall* be free!

Lay the proud usurpers low!
Tyrants fall in ev'ry foe!
Liberty's in ev'ry blow!—
Let us do—or die!

Robert Burns.